Bt
3.60

D1253939

Southern Fiction Today: RENASCENCE AND BEYOND

Southern Fiction
Today: RENASCENCE
AND BEYOND

EDITED BY
GEORGE CORE

University of Georgia Press
ATHENS

Preface

Iт is a pleasure to record the various debts which I have incurred in the making of this book. First and foremost, I want to thank the contributors for their splendid essays—and for coming to Davidson College to give the Reynolds Lectures in March of this year. It was a fine occasion which I remember with delight, and I believe that the first Reynolds Symposium proved a success in a way that the fact of publication confirms only distantly. This record does not show, for example, that Hugh Holman lectured brilliantly to a group of undergraduates on the major novels of William Faulkner—or that Louis Rubin lectured equally well on local color fiction to another large class. Nor does it show that Walter Sullivan read a chapter from his new novel with great felicity for a large and appreciative audience. I wish to thank these gentlemen—especially Mr. Holman who acted as field marshal for the occasion by conducting most of the correspondence involved while I served as his adjutant.

It was good of the Reynolds Committee at Davidson College to approve my proposal concerning the symposium, and in this connection I am particularly grateful to James S. Purcell, chairman of the English department, who warmly endorsed my recommendations and who helped in various ways with the conduct of affairs.

The Z. Smith Reynolds Foundation has not only my gratitude but that of the student body and faculty at Davidson as well for its continuing financial support of the lecture programs at the college. Many distinguished men have come to Davidson College through the generosity of this foundation, and a number of fine lectures have been presented there in the course of the past several years. One hopes that the yearly programs will hereafter include a symposium.

I know that I speak for the contributors when I say all of us are particularly grateful to Mr. LeRoy Percy for his innumerable kind offices and to my wife Susan for her gracious hospitality. Susan and I in turn owe a considerable debt to Mr. and Mrs. Norman Johnson for their cordial help.

I want to express my appreciation to Mrs. Agnes Kuentzel for typing the transcript of the symposium proper, "The State of Southern Fiction," and to Mrs. Sarah Penland for preparing and overseeing the final typescript of the book as a whole.

The dedication of this volume to the late Professor Donald Davidson ends my acknowledgements on a sad note. All of us shall miss him—a distinguished poet, critic, scholar, and teacher who made so many contributions to Southern letters that it is impossible to list them here. Suffice it to say that his was one of the most searching and unflinching visions that has come forth in the South during this century. Hugh Holman, Louis Rubin, Walter Sullivan, and George Core dedicate *Southern Fiction Today* to the memory of Donald Davidson.

George Core

August 1968
Athens, Georgia

To the Memory of Donald Davidson (1893–1968)

Introduction BY C. HUGH HOLMAN

THERE CAN BE LITTLE QUESTION of the success of Southern writing in the twentieth century. To demonstrate that success in fields as varied as poetry, drama, criticism, history, and fiction, it is necessary only to name a few writers whose absence from the rolls of contemporary American letters would so drastically change the picture of our national literature in the second third of the twentieth century that it is almost unimaginable that they should not be there. Among these names we certainly should list William Faulkner, Thomas Wolfe, Robert Penn Warren, Ellen Glasgow, Flannery O'Connor, Allen Tate, Donald Davidson, John Crowe Ransom, Caroline Gordon, Katherine Anne Porter, Carson McCullers, Eudora Welty, Douglas Southall Freeman, Erskine Caldwell, Paul Green, Lillian Hellman, Tennessee Williams and William Styron. This list not only could be extended almost indefinitely, but I am sure that the reader is squirming inwardly at some of the omissions which I have made and that seem to him inexcusable.

To say these things is merely to say again that Southern literature in the twentieth century has earned a permanent place in the chronicles of American literary history. The question with which Mr. Rubin, Mr. Sullivan, and I are concerned in this symposium, however, is not the question of the intrinsic value of this literature. All of us accept that value. It is the question of the continuing relevance of literature written in and based on this region to the life and times of the South and the Nation.

May I suggest that almost all of us who have studied a literature course in recent years have felt in one sense, at least, the powerful impact of the Southern renascence, as we usually call this movement; for most of us have been taught the careful analysis of a literary work in and of itself, the study of its formal characteristics, and the attempt to evaluate its metaphors, its images, and its symbols. We have been taught that the primary value of a work of art is a function of the authority with which it still can speak directly to us, and that the task of the reader and the critic is the task of looking at that work itself and evaluating it as a successful or unsuccessful artifact in a world of objective realities. The extent to which this critical approach to literature has conquered the classrooms of America and has enriched and enhanced the study of literature for college students all over our nation is one measure of the relevance of an aspect of the Southern renascence. The widespread acceptance of that method is a triumph for the New Critics, and the New Critics are essentially the Vanderbilt Fugitives and Agrarians, and through their efforts—especially those of Robert Penn Warren and Cleanth Brooks—they have changed the doctrine for teaching literature in American colleges and schools.

But there are other questions of relevance than the literary ones. There are the question of whether the writer dealing with Southern material is dealing with a real world whose immediate problems confront us from day to day and the question of whether he brings to these problems an illumination which makes the paths which we must travel easier and helps us toward making intelligent decisions. Furthermore, the issue of whether he is pointing us to the questions which should be asked about our society is also highly relevant. In these respects, the Southern writer tends to be a social critic, a portrayer of a region, a pointer to its social ills, a suggester of means for their correction.

The South in the period after the Civil War and Reconstruction was a poverty-stricken and debilitated region possessed of an enormous problem having to do in part with a newly-liberated mass of former slaves. In its various turnings and twistings in efforts to find resolutions to poverty, to depletion, and to the problem of the Negro citizen, it took many and often devious courses, some of which we can today view only with alarm and a sense of guilt received as an inheritance from our ancestors. I think that the literature of the South in the last two-thirds of the century has emphasized the nature of these problems, has portrayed sometimes in coruscating detail the nature and quality of life among the poor whites, of life among the Negroes in the ghettos, of life in the slums, of life in the shacks and on tenant farms, of life in the kitchens and crowded bedrooms of sharecroppers. To the extent that it has kept us aware of what lies around us and has stirred up our social consciences to the obligations which we as citizens bear for all the men who are about us, this literature has had a high relevance. And it is difficult to read much of the writing which has been produced about the South since 1920 without being forced to look again at a series of social issues of tremendous magnitude. The extent to which the writers, sometimes angry and sometimes anguished, have pointed to these ills within the body politic of the Southeastern United States is a measure of the success which they have had in becoming a significant part of the growth and development of the health and sanity of the region they and we inhabit.

But literature has another relevance than that of the accurate depiction of the present scene or the enunciation of its soluble or insoluble problems. That dimension is one of moral, ethical, and cosmic truth, and I believe that it is in this particular respect that the writers of the Southern renascence have made their major contribution to the literature of the world. They have seen in the tragic history of the South a pattern of man's imperfections, an example of Americans living under duress, of Americans living under difficulties, of Americans to whom defeat was knowledge brought painfully to the heart, of Americans who had to accept the impossibility of tasks which they wanted desperately to do. In the high-flying optimism which has characterized the rest of the American nation through much of its history, the South has been a separate pocket whose historical experience was one of tragic defeat. Southern writers in our time have found that tragic history a metaphor for the fate of man in his world, and out of that history they have fashioned a lesson with deep moral and ethical significance for men everywhere. They have brought the experience of the South as example and as inspiration to the larger nation suddenly discovering in this century of war, fear, and turmoil that all is not perfect on this globe or even in the Western Hemisphere.

Southern writers by and large have retained a religious sense of man, or, if not a religious sense, at least a sense of man's potential, of his responsibility, and of his innate dignity. They have been able to fashion from the Southern experience a literature which translates man's dreams and goals and his failures to achieve them into something resembling tragic grandeur, and they have given that literature as a positive note in an otherwise despairing and nihilistic twentieth century. If we believe that a tragic vision of life, an ethical view of experience, and a responsible and dignified view of man have relevance for the world, the nation, and our region, then the literature of the modern South has great relevance for all of us.

The question, however, remains of how much of the literature of the South of the present day and of tomorrow is or will be in this unique sense relevant in a changing world where, as Vann Woodward once remarked, in the race between the bulldozer and the magnolia tree, the bulldozer is clearly winning, where industrialism is replacing agriculture, where cities are replacing small towns, and where hamlets are becoming shopping centers. Does the region still prove to be a fruitful subject for a literature which can speak to problems that are deeply meaningful to the citizens of the South and the Nation? It is with that question that we shall concern ourselves in this symposium, first, by examining what the literature has been since 1920, and then by speculating on its possibilities for continuing relevance in a world of rapid social and economic change.

Contents

The New Faustus: THE SOUTHERN RENASCENCE AND THE JOYCEAN AESTHETIC
WALTER SULLIVAN

I WANT TO BEGIN with a brief discussion of two novels: *An Exile* by Madison Jones and *The Confessions of Nat Turner* by William Styron. *An Exile* is the story of Hank Tawes, sheriff of a rural Southern county, a man of reasonable competence and absolute honesty, whose worst problem at the beginning of the book is a nagging wife. In the course of the narrative, Tawes is seduced by the daughter of a moonshiner, and thereby he becomes a party to a violation of the law that he has sworn to uphold. Stern consequences follow: Tawes' marriage breaks up, one of his associates is killed as a result of his complicity, and, in the end, though the murderous moonshiners are to be brought to justice, Tawes pays with his life. The moral is clear, and the book, like all of Jones' work, is full of bucolic imagery, of sequences flagrantly calculated to show the evil of urbanization and the questionable nature of material progress. In many significant ways Jones is a neo-Agrarian and *An Exile* is a neo-Agrarian book.

Styron, like Jones, is a Southerner, forty-three-years old, and like Jones, he has published four novels, but here the similarity between them seems to end. Jones is a political conservative, Styron, a liberal. Jones' prose is workmanlike, sometimes stolid, but always functional and concrete. Styron is lyrical, his language is frequently beautiful, and he exhibits a tendency to overwrite. To Jones the South is rural middle Tennessee, to Styron it is Tidewater Virginia. Jones is Calvinist, Styron is existentialist, though neither is purely that; and superficially at least, *The Confessions of Nat Turner* and *An Exile* are about as different as any two books could possibly be.

Nat Turner is, of course, the story of the slave insurrection of 1831, the events that led up to the bloodshed, the executions that followed. But as Styron tells us in an introduction, *Nat Turner* is not so much an historical novel as it is a "meditation on history" which perhaps accounts for the book's episodic structure and its anachronistic tone. The narrative follows Nat from his earliest memory to the moment before his death: we are brought to see his relationships with various white owners and overseers: we watch the development of his urgent need for vengeance—or is it atonement, expiation, this terrible necessity for the spilling of the white man's blood? We literally see the heads roll, and after the carnage we wait with Nat in his cell, listening to his final words, remembering, trying, along with him, to discover why. Whether or not the book is successful, whatever we and those who follow us may think of it ten or twenty or fifty or a hundred years from now, one thing seems certain: Styron wrote with his eye on the present and not on the past.

So this account based on the history of more than a century ago roots itself firmly in the here and now, and Jones' novel which is contemporary looks wistfully backwards, and in their distinctions and contradictions, the two novels would seem roughly to establish the limits within which all Southern fiction is bound to fall. But a closer examination of the two works tends to demonstrate otherwise: it is my judgment that at their profoundest levels, *An Exile* and *Nat Turner* are expressions of a single hopelessness, a thrust toward destruction, the tired and jaded soul's longing for death.

Consider, in this light, the key scene in *An Exile*, the moment about which all the consequences of the narrative turn. When the sheriff stops an automobile for what begins as a routine investigation, the young driver abandons the vehicle leaving his female passenger to deal with the sheriff, and Tawes knows immediately what he has stumbled upon. The car is used for running moonshine, the tank under the back seat is doubtless full of whisky at this very moment; and the girl is more cheap than pretty, more forward than seductive: Jones draws her vividly in terms of tawdry hair ribbon and floral perfume. There is no earthly reason why the sheriff should be so taken with her that he would fail to do his duty. He has never seen her before and his character has been established as that of a responsible, not a sensual or impulsive, man. Yet, in the twinkling of an eye, he abandons everything—duty, family, personal honor—and if Jones meant for us to infer that the sheriff's decision was a product of his lust, then the hero is not worthy of our sorrow and the ensuing anger and agony do not signify.

But the girl is only a catalyst, a superficial reason that allows the sheriff to pursue a grim and deeper course. For Tawes sees, as Jones does, that a general debauchery has already overtaken the world. The landscape has been transformed, the woods have been cut, the streams have been defiled and the air has been polluted. Traditional values have been ridiculed into desuetude, religion has been stripped of its mysteries by modern theology, and both public and private institutions have fallen into decay. What the sheriff seeks within this frame is not success or honesty or sexual fulfilment or even the exercise of charity, but rather the peace that follows upon self-destruction. He wants out of a world that has been turned hideous by its loss of a sense of moral values, and the girl is his opportunity: she furnishes him the means. With intractable purpose, Tawes strips himself of the old loyalties which might deter him: he seeks guilt as a gentler soul might gather flowers, and thereby motivates and accrues significance for his own end. In Madison Jones' canon, Tawes is no exception: this is the way Jones sees the plight of modern man.

And so it is with Styron. Nat Turner lives in another time

and works out his destiny under a vastly different set of circumstances and presents to us a face of another color, but he and Sheriff Tawes are nonetheless brothers under the skin. As is the case with Tawes, on the surface what Turner is and what Turner ultimately does will not jibe. As Styron draws him for us, Nat Turner is intelligent, perceptive, capable, consumed with hatred for white people, but kind and loyal to his Negro friends. He survives and even thrives under certain of his masters because he is not only a mechanic of great skill, an inventor, and therefore a valuable property, but he is a master of human relations, a shrewd psychologist who knows how to deal with his oppressors, an accomplished dissembler who possesses monumental self-control. He is an idealization rather than a realistic portrayal, an exaggerated composite of many splendid human qualities, and as such, he jars violently against what Styron finally has him do. I do not mean that I find his hate for his masters unmotivated or that one would not expect him, sooner or later, to shed white blood. But the insurrection had no hope of success, and whatever the real Nat Turner might have foreseen in this connection, Styron's Nat Turner would have had to know from the outset that what he planned was doom. Perhaps it can be argued that his willingness to sacrifice his friends was evidence of his heroic stature, that only a figure of tragic proportions would see the necessity for leading those he loved to a blood-letting that was bound to terminate in their own deaths. But this is not the point I wish to make or to refute.

It is germane to my interpretation of the novel that once the insurrection has started, Turner finds himself unable to kill. His axe will not strike the flesh toward which he directs it: his muscles will not move to destroy at his brain's command. The single murder that he is able to perpetrate is that of Margaret Whitehead, and this is not vengeance at all, but an act of love. He is leaving a world which has grown unworthy for human habitation and he will take her with him, and it is she whom he thinks about later just before he dies.

4

What we are dealing with, then, is not the old Nat Turner of our shameful history, but a new creation, a man with a voice that is insistently modern and therefore insistently hopeless: he is one with the *personae* in the plays of LeRoi Jones: his spirit is that of Stokely Carmichael and Rap Brown. In a world too far depraved to be reformed, he has given up all expectation of being delivered from oppression: he desires now only to destroy and to be destroyed. On these terms, the novel makes sense. And on these terms, Madison Jones and William Styron, Sheriff Tawes and Nat Turner meet, though they began their journeys at opposite poles. In a faithless universe, all our heroes wish for death. Why should this be? How did our literature, and by inference our society, come to this?

In an effort to shed some light on those questions, I want to turn to James Joyce, not to *Ulysses,* which has had such an extravagant influence on the twentieth-century novel, but to *A Portrait of the Artist as a Young Man,* which seems to me to be partly a prophecy of what we as people and as writers are becoming and partly a description of what we have already become. *A Portrait* has been too widely read to require recapitulation. As everyone knows, it is the story of young Stephen Dedalus, which is to say, James Joyce, who grows up, goes to school, reads, writes, sins, repents, considers becoming a priest, and finally, in the climactic epiphany scene, discovers that his destiny is to follow his mythical namesake, to become a maker, a writer, and, as he puts it, "to recreate life out of life!"[1]

Now, *A Portrait* has a very curious structure. Since the time of Jane Austen, almost all novels have been built according to the same general pattern. The first two-thirds or three-quarters of the narrative are devoted to an introduction of the characters and the elements of the plot, a statement of theme, and a development of all these to a point of maximum complication. Here the story begins its run toward its conclusion: dramatic tension increases as the plot unwinds: the writer's style tightens up, and though he may put in a hold here and there to keep his momentum from carrying him too rapidly toward the end, the time for digressions and the introduction of new material—not to mention philosophizing—is soon over.

In *A. Portrait,* the epiphany scene occurs almost exactly two-thirds of the way through the novel. It is a climax, a peak of Stephen's spiritual life, and therefore the reader would ordinarily expect the narrative to turn here and to start toward its denouement. But the opposite takes place: there follow a number of conversations between Stephen and members of his family, Davin, the dean, a group of students, Lynch, Cranly. The old rejections which are the meat of the first two-thirds of the book are taken up once more. Stephen will not learn Gaelic, or join the Irish revolutionary party, or sign the Tzar's petition for universal peace. Finally, there is a discussion of aesthetic theory before the story reaches the highly dramatic material of Stephen's total rejection of the church.

What this unusual structure proves first of all is that there are no absolute rules which writers must follow: one can do anything if he is good enough and Joyce was. But beyond this, there is the question of emphasis, of whether, given the novel's construction, our primary concern should be with Stephen's discovering that he wants to be an artist, or rather with his determination, once he has made this discovery, that he will achieve competence, that he will gain skill at whatever cost. There is, I think, a tendency on the part of modern readers to see in *A Portrait* what we take to be a natural and largely unmitigable relationship of epiphany and exile. We assume that, since Stephen wants to be a writer, it is therefore imperative that he free his mind and his temperament from all feeling and thought that are not purely artistic. He must abandon his family and leave Ireland to keep from being annoyed by them, to preserve himself from the demands they might make on his time and energy. He is, we think, right to break with the church, right to fear "the chemical action which would be set up in his soul by a false homage to a symbol behind which are massed twenty centuries of authority and veneration."[2] We conceive his only duty, his only loyalty to be to his art, and in seeing him in this way, we do not deviate greatly from the world's conventional concept of the generic artist.

But a closer reading of A Portrait and particularly a more attentive examination of its structure might lead us to another conclusion. Joseph Frank and others have shown how modern novelists manipulate form in order to bring the various parts of their narratives into more meaningful juxtapositions. Where scenes are placed in a novel, how the novel is put together are very important indeed, and it was neither chance nor ignorance that induced Joyce to place his discussion of aesthetics where the reader would expect to find a passage of dramatic action, nor was he careless in throwing repeated emphasis on Stephen's rejection of religion and in using this rejection as the ultimate climax of the book. My point is that a proper interpretation of the novel must see the rejections not as ordinary and predictable consequences of an artistic ambition, but as free choices consciously selected and deliberately made. Ever solicitous of the role he plays, Stephen strikes a pose of Satanic majesty. "I will not serve,"[3] he tells Cranly, echoing Lucifer. And though he no longer believes, he does not completely disbelieve, and he is prepared to pay the terrible price that his apostacy might exact. "I will tell you also what I do not fear," he says. "I am not afraid to make a mistake, even a great mistake, a lifelong mistake and perhaps as long as eternity too."[4] For the sake of his art and his competence therein, he will risk damnation.

It would be going too far to say that A Portrait is a twentieth-century version of the Faustus legend. I know of no evidence that Joyce intended any such thing, but the parallels between the old necromancer and the young Dedalus are sufficiently striking not to be ignored. Faustus—I think now of Marlowe's traditional version—traded his soul to the devil for a power that he found himself increasingly unable to use properly. The story, as its continuing appeal to writers of all sorts attests, has many facets. It is a monument to the vanity of man, it is indicative of man's demonic proclivities: and the playing out of the narrative invariably involves an assault upon established order, both transcendent and mundane. One of the remarkable aspects of *A Portrait* is the manner in which Joyce is able to develop Stephen's pride to the point that it becomes a dynamic force in the book. Like Faustus, he considers himself spiritually and intellectually superior to the common run of humanity, and it is this phase of his character, not weakness of the flesh or his talents and competencies, that furnishes the basic motivations for the drama and makes the novel work. To be sure, in the strict sense, Stephen, unlike Faustus, has no direct commerce with the devil, and indeed, he thinks probably that the devil does not exist. But should he exist, Stephen has delivered himself knowingly into his hands. Finally, and most significantly, for the sake of increased literary power, i.e. his own kind of magic, Stephen abandons the sources of political and social and metaphysical order with results in many ways similar to those that Faustus achieved.

At the beginning of Marlowe's play, when Faustus is first succumbing to the temptations of his own vanity, he casts himself in the role of benefactor of mankind. He will change the landscape, alter political structures and otherwise alleviate the problems of the human state. But the course of his use of power is one long decline, and he is reduced finally to the perpetration of empty exhibitions and practical jokes. In the general dissipation of his morality, he becomes petty, vindictive, dishonest. At the last, he is insensitive to the suffering he once meant to assuage, and the power for which he traded his soul has grown maleficent in his hands. It will be considered literary heresy, I know, but I submit that something of the same thing happened to Joyce.

A Portrait ends at just exactly the right place. The great rejections have been made: the full weight of them, what they mean, what they imply is clear: Stephen's courage in setting out on his own is gloriously realized. But Stephen and Joyce go on, Stephen into *Ulysses,* Joyce to the remaining days and years of his life, all of them devoted to, revolving totally around, his own literary ambition. It is, of course, a risky business to equate what is made with the maker, the character with the author, but in this case, the risk is well taken: Joyce is Stephen: Stephen is Joyce. It is also true that the character of Stephen in *Ulysses* amends in certain particulars the Stephen of *A Portrait.* And Joyce insisted that the word *Young* was the key to his title, thus implying that both he and Stephen had subsequently changed. Unquestionably they did, but the rejections remained inviolate. Joyce was almost symbolically tardy in regularizing his relationship with Nora, his animosity toward Ireland continued unabated, and he died beyond the sacraments of the church.

All of this is important to us for a number of reasons. First, the power Joyce dealt for in his rejection of the sources of order served him no better than, in an earlier day, it had served Faustus. From the magnificence of his previous achievement, particularly in "The Dead" and in *A Portrait* itself, Joyce's subsequent career was a decline through largely empty experimentation into what for all practical purposes can only be called the meaninglessness of *Finnegans Wake.* I am aware, as I have already indicated, of the great influence that *Ulysses* has exerted on the form of the novel. Its authority is everywhere to be felt. No one works outside its vast hegemony. But influence is one thing and accomplishment is something else. Often they are coincident: as often they are not: in art, as in science, the pioneer will not necessarily produce the finished product. I do not think *Ulysses* is a good book. It is intellectually a masterpiece: it is fraught with breath-taking stylistic accomplishments. But it is an empty novel. In spite of all its truly impressive technique, it has no moral center. The Molly Bloom soliloquy, celebrated as it is, is tantamount to Faustus' plucking fruit in the dead of winter.

There would be nothing to fear from all this, if we, like Marlowe's audiences, saw Faustus not only as tragic protagonist, but as a cautionary figure, a warning of what will happen to us if we follow in his footsteps. But on the contrary, two generations of artists and intellectuals have seen Stephen Dedalus solely as hero, and they have viewed his rejections as elements in a legitimate quest for artistic freedom which should be emulated by all. On the campus, in publishing houses, in workshops and symposia and theaters and libraries, Stephen Dedalus has become our folk hero. Which is to say, in the modern literary community, Faustus has become Everyman. We too have abandoned all loyalty to family, state, and the substantive forms of religion. We have even taken the next logical step: the active pursuit of disorder has become an end to the extent that we perpetrate revolt on almost every level, not for a redress of real grievances, but for the sake of establishing the anarchy that has become our goal. We interdict our mental processes by drugs; we acknowledge the meaningless mouthing of any hairy exhibitionist to be legitimate poetry; as Philip Rahv has pointed out, we choose our saints from the ranks of moral idiots such as Jean Genet. Our novelists write of anti-heroes—disorder again—who live by the premise that there is no such thing as right and wrong. Or take the case of William Burroughs. Not content with the confusion that is native to his obscene tracts, he shuffles his pages and jumbles his lines after his manuscripts are finished, and he is praised by Norman Mailer and Mary McCarthy and hundreds of others who ought to know better for the beauty and—mark the word—the *freedom* he has brought to art. We try to salve our consciences by violent partisanship and a staunch devotion to selected and intellectually popular causes, but by any measure that is applicable, we continue in our spiritual and ethical decline.

And we shall not be saved by our enhanced literary competence. Technique and style are not sufficient: words, no matter how beautifully they are put together, are not enough.

But in many cases, words are all we have, and thus we witness a new school of literary endeavor: the novel about the novel, or about style, or about language, or meaning, or the novel that is a burlesque of itself. This is literature that ceases to signify in any recognizable sense, and which degenerates into elaborate connundrums and extended puns. This is what Joyce predicted and in a way made possible for us. And it is against this background that I should like to examine the Southern renascence.

The reasons that are usually given for the flowering of Southern literature in the decades following World War I are sufficiently familiar to us now that we need not dwell on them. We are told that the South was a homogenous society: that it knew the meaning of defeat and suffering, having lost the Civil War: that it was agrarian in its basic orientation and therefore in tune with nature and with the particular view of reality that a knowledge of and dependence on the seasons is likely to impose. Southern society was said to be religious—or more specifically Protestant—conservative, and blessed with the ability, according to Richard Weaver, to understand that the whole of a thing was greater than the sum of its parts. The South was impoverished and cursed with a class system—the Negro at the bottom—which may or may not have been a good thing for literature, depending on which critic you prefer. The Southerner saw the world and its history as a series of images, rather than as a sweep of theories, which is to say that his vision was not abstract, but concrete. And finally, for my summation, the Southern artist saw that the traditional society in which he lived and about which he wrote was on the verge of dissolution: he struck his chronicle of it in the twilight of its going.

I suppose at this point it is hardly necessary for me to say that although I recognize and even urge the validity of all the foregoing reasons for the renascence, it is the last—should I call it the *Gotterdammerung* theory?—which most appeals to me. I know the dangers of substantive criticism: I am fully aware, I think, that if we begin to judge literature by the attitudes it reflects, by what it says, rather than how it says it, we are opening a Pandora's box of frightening dimensions. We are exposing ourselves to a score of illegitimate ideological claims and romantic excesses. But there is no easy or absolute way to assess literary merit. There is no critical method which does not involve risk. An evaluation of the theme, along with the moral outlook, the world view, the metaphysical view from which the author writes, is ultimately necessary. There are many books technically more perfect than *War and Peace* and *Don Quixote*. *A Portrait of the Artist as a Young Man* is one of them. But who would dare say that *A Portrait* is on the same plane with these two masterpieces?

So I see the set of values which prevailed in the South during the twenties and thirties as at least a *sine qua non,* if not the major source of the literary renascence. Other American writers, from other sections of the country, were also writing well, and it is not mere coincidence that the best of them were dealing with the decline of accustomed belief: Hemingway in *The Sun Also Rises* and *A Farewell to Arms,* Fitzgerald in *The Great Gatsby,* Dos Passos in *U.S.A.,* and there were others. But in the South the traditional society with its traditional values was more fully intact, and because the South had been isolated for the previous half century or more, its confrontation with the post-war disillusionment was more dramatic. This, along with the other characteristics and circumstances which have been set forth, was the ground out of which the original renascence developed.

Now, the old society with its old views is, if not dead, so far weakened that it is no longer viable in a literary sense. The Southern outlook is no longer agrarian: Southerners as a whole are no longer pious or respectful of tradition: and the fabric of Southern life—which now is largely bourgeois life—changes every day. And the South has suffered the common alienation. Unlike Faulkner who during the thirties hunted and fished and drank with a cross-section of the people in and around Oxford, the typical contemporary Southern artist is so far divorced in attitude and temperament from the ordinary citizen that the two cannot meet without falling out: and frequently the Southern artist eschews Southern society totally and goes to live in a more congenial place such as Roxbury, Connecticut. Finally, the Southern writer or intellectual is as conformist in his ethical and aesthetic dispositions as the artists and intellectuals of New York or California or New Mexico.

It is my judgment that the novels and poems being written today, in the South as elsewhere, are not as good as those which were written in the twenties and thirties. I do not think they are apt to be as good until we are able to bring ourselves to a new iconoclasm. We must, somehow, destroy the notions that order is bad, that technique is all, that aesthetics furnish a sufficient code of life, and that picketing the courthouse or the corner cafe are the sole requisites for ethical fulfilment. This is not to say, as I doubtless will be accused of saying, that we must turn back. We cannot turn back any more than we can raise the dead or stop the sun or part the ocean. We are where we are in history and the past is past: nor can we pretend that the old society exists or that we are products of it. We will have to find our own way out. As individual writers, we will have to discover our own sources of moral organization.

Which is what Flannery O'Connor did. She brought to the old Southern images her strict devotion to her Roman Catholic God and her fully developed sense of a universe which operates under the terms of His provenance. The social disintegrations that she portrayed in her books are all measured against her sense of good and evil. Her fiction was full of her knowledge of the destiny of man according to Christian eschatology. And in her best work, the clash of angelic and demonic forces is clearly present. Therefore, when Tarwater baptizes the retarded child Bishop and drowns him in the process, we are dealing with something more than mere Southern grotesque: the scene achieves a significance that extends, without mimicking, the last pages of *The Sound and the Fury*.

Thus Flannery O'Connor has shown us one way to make what remains of the Southern experience and landscape the vital literary materials that they used to be. There are doubtless other paths back toward a sense of morality and the stability of order. But for the moment, at least, I do not think they are likely to be social. I do not conceive of finding in the near future a sufficient authority in the image of the family or the image of the state or in the images of the organizations and movements to which we pledge our loyalties, the frame of regularity within which we can work out the deviations which are our art. I do not say that in order to write we must all become Roman Catholics. But we must become *something*: we must see the world as larger than ourselves or our generation or our ability to send a space ship to the moon.

And I am finally optimistic: I believe that beyond this present lull in the renascence there is the possibility of renewed fruition. Perhaps in spite of what we have done to ourselves and to our environment, we in the South, alone of all people, have by virtue of God's grace or by Malthusian accident, enough remaining of what went into the old renascence to furnish material to the themes and impulses of the new. We shall never again be agrarian. But our cities will never be as large as New York or Los Angeles. And because we have come to them later and under different circumstances, we see the urban experience in a different light. We have left to us something of the old sense of character, which is to say, we continue to view people as individuals, and our gifts for narrative, and for taking the concrete view, are not totally dead. They await our rediscovery. But we must continue to remind ourselves that this will not occur as a result of some general enlightenment. In terms of mundane history, each of us is alone to an extent that even Joyce never dreamed of. And each of us will have to escape the new Faustus in his own way.

NOTES

1. *Portrait of the Artist as a Young Man* (New York, 1964), p. 239.
2. *Ibid.*, p. 243.
3. *Ibid.*, p. 246.
4. *Ibid.*, p. 247.

The View
from the Regency-Hyatt:
SOUTHERN SOCIAL ISSUES
AND THE OUTER WORLD
C. HUGH HOLMAN

THE interpretation of Southern culture and Southern literature
has suffered from absolutism almost as much as it has from
sentimental adulation and from vindictive enmity. Usually in
the minds of each of its critics, whether of its life or its letters,
there is a monolithic South, but early and late few of these
monoliths have been very much like the others. Yet, the fact
that individual concepts of the region are remarkably varied
does not alter the monistic tendency that calls them all into
being. Let us review briefly some of the most obvious of these
absolutist views.

There is the aristocratic South of broad lawns, great trees,
tall, white columns, and happy banjo-strumming Negroes. This
is the old South of Thomas Nelson Page of Virginia and, more
recently, it is the South of Stark Young of Mississippi and, to
a certain extent, of Margaret Mitchell of Atlanta. It managed
to survive the destruction of war and the abolition of slavery
without losing its good manners or its sense of honor and
without soiling its damask linen—although that linen is growing increasingly threadbare.

There is also a South which became an apocalyptic vision
in which one sees arrested forever beneath lurid skies a blasted

Gothic landscape, wherein Simon Legree alternates between lusting after the slave girl Cassy and beating Uncle Tom to death. This is the South of the abolition societies, although it is actually not the South of Mrs. Stowe herself, despite the fact that she created its most enduring metaphors in *Uncle Tom's Cabin*. It is also the South of many of the modern reconstructionists and has been at least once, in *Band of Angels,* that of Robert Penn Warren.

There is a South of industrialization, liberalism, and all the middle-class democratic virtues, a South which is primarily viewed as a problem in the management of society, its natural resources, and its people. This South was announced by Henry Grady of Atlanta and documented by Howard Odum and his cohorts at Chapel Hill, and it is still a very lively ideal in both these places. There is also a South that represents a special and feverishly deceitful state of mind torn between dreams of past grandeur and a sense of guilt. This South was most clearly defined by W. J. Cash of Charlotte, but it has frequently been echoed since the publication of Cash's brilliant book, *The Mind of the South,* in 1941.

There is a South that is a degenerate, poverty-stricken world—a land of people ill-housed, ill-clothed, and ill-fed, wherein economic deprivation and cultural illiteracy combined with despair to produce utter hopelessness and violence. This South has remarkable similarities to many of the pictures that are currently being painted of the ghettos in our great cities and it may be achieving a new relevance in our tormented world. It is the South of Mark Twain's river towns, of Franklin Delano Roosevelt's economic programs, of Erskine Caldwell's Georgia uplands, and of William Faulkner's Snopeses and Bundrens.

And there is also a South which is a lost paradise of order and stability, of honor and a religious view of man. This South is a challenge, an ideal, and a star by which to steer, even though the mariners themselves admit that it really is a light never seen on land or sea. This is the South of the Vanderbilt

Agrarians, a South which has proved to be a powerfully dynamic symbol of agrarian opposition to capitalistic industrialism. It has been magnificently celebrated in some of the best poetry and fiction of the region as a repository of the finest traditions of the old South.

Each of these monistic concepts is true within its own limits, and each is false as a picture of the entire region. For each of these concepts has been an attempt to bind together a heterogeneous land and a varied people through the application of a Procrustean model made of monistic and simplistic—although often highly sophisticated—generalizations.

It seems to me that my eminent colleague and dear friend, Walter Sullivan, has argued in this symposium for still another monolithic approach to an aspect of Southern culture. He cogently stated the case for what I believe to be a special aspect of the Southern experience, an aspect peculiarly amenable to a highly sophisticated and self-conscious literary technique, basically that of James Joyce. To me, his argument for the existence of his South and its special literary resurgence was convincing. The famed Southern renascence would have been a lesser thing by far had the movement that Mr. Sullivan describes not occurred, and, indeed, had it not found expression in novels, such as his own and Louis D. Rubin's. Yet, as a pluralist and as one who believes that there are many Souths with many histories and many problems, I should like to suggest that there are other strings to the literary bow which sped the arrow of this renascence and that, though perhaps of coarser and less-enduring fiber than the one that Mr. Sullivan has described, they were of importance to the development of Southern letters in the second third of this century and can be ignored in a serious examination of what Southern literature has been like in the days of its glory and is likely to be tomorrow only at the peril of dangerous incompleteness.

The occurrence of genius, even of high talent, is always finally inexplicable. Who would have dreamed that Stratford would produce a Shakespeare and, yet, as Matthew Arnold has observed in "The Function of Criticism at the Present Time," the proper cultural and intellectual climate must exist if genius is to flourish and truly realize itself in significant art. Shakespeare did leave Stratford and did find among the dramatists and poets of the first Elizabeth's London a cultural and artistic environment conducive to the fruitful working of his genius. I think the South in our century has had many elements which have made it a promising field for the serious artist. For all its divergence within itself, for all the varied Souths, there is still a geographical region that has certain common and easily recognized qualities which set it apart from the rest of the nation. Among those qualities, I believe, these are of special importance: the presence of the Negro and the shame of his enslavement and his disenfranchisement; an agricultural economy; the historical experience of military defeat, military occupation, and reconstruction. The union of this body of experience as subject matter and a passionate concern in terms of the region with a great many men of marked literary talent produced a period rich in works of literary art.

But literary works have literary as well as social contexts, and they possess the miraculous ability to grow by feeding upon themselves. The existence of a substantial body of serious writing is a requisite—or at least a substantial encouragement—to any literary movement of importance. Such a burgeoning of writing—good, bad and mediocre—in poetry, in drama, in criticism, and particularly in fiction, began to occur in the 1920s. It had many sources. After the First World War, as Allen Tate has suggested, the South made a belated entry into the modern world.[1] Mr. Tate is impressed—and properly—with the backward look which the South cast at its own past in this moment of transition, and he sees that look as the central energy of the renascence. The tragic history of the South made it a vital metaphor for the war-torn and disillusioned twentieth century in which its crucial and frustrating experiences began to speak with remarkable directness to the entire nation which, except for the South, had been oblivious to the human potential for disaster and had believed itself immune to permanent defeat. In our time, as there was not for the rest of the nation in the nineteenth century, there is deep meaning in witnessing the symbolic act of biting the bullet. But more occurred than merely a looking backward into history; for this time, the South also began looking around and looking at itself and no longer solely through the rose-colored glasses of sentiment or the defensive blinders of a lost cause, and the contemporary condition of the region could, and it still does, also speak with immediacy and authority to its artists.

This condition was in many parts of the South one of bone-gnawing poverty and endless defeat. It rested on depleted soil, deflated markets, dilapidated buildings, and debilitating malnutrition. It was a reflection of a vicious tenant-farming and sharecropping system, a most rudimentary educational system for the underprivileged, and an intense emotion-charged, pietistic, fundamentalist, non-theological religion that expressed itself in grotesqueries such as snake-handling and speaking with tongues. These conditions were as much a part of the subject matter of the Southern renascence as were the history of the region or the humor of its retreating frontier or the dream of the days of its baronial glory. They also formed a subject which could deeply engage the moral and social conscience of the author. And Southern writers who took this subject usually applied to it a socio-literary method which was essentially that of critical social realism, and this method should be added to—certainly not substituted for—the tradition which Mr. Sullivan has so admirably described, and I should add parenthetically that his and mine together do not cover or exhaust the field of the South as a subject inspiring to writers of talent.

In the 1920s, 1930s, and the early 1940s, the work of Sinclair Lewis as social critic and satirist, as the coruscating portrayer and diagnostician of a society lacking in values and the bases of a good life, was at least quantitatively as important to Southern writing as that of James Joyce. Certainly, the brash iconoclasm of H. L. Mencken was echoed fully as often as the Tory tones of T. S. Eliot. While many writers did seek in themselves the answers to their own riddles and to the riddles of their world, many others saw in the outside world a challenging subject for portrayal and criticism.

And one of the generating forces for the renascence was the energy of this social anger and regional criticism. It rose from a skeptical look at the legend of the Old South—as, indeed, the early *Fugitive* movement had—from a distaste for sentimentality—which characteristic was almost a hallmark of the renascence—and from a clear-eyed surveillance of the region in terms of its weaknesses and its suffering. Behind this analysis of the present was a sense of the past and a reverence for the dignity of man, but it expressed itself in anger and protest. Jeeter Lester, in *Tobacco Road,* is a shiftless, hopeless, and helpless man, but there echo in his vacant brain thoughts that rest on other days and other ways and he abides by a faithfulness to the soil which, in his case, is both insane and self-serving but is also real. As Caldwell said, "They had so much faith in nature . . . that they could not understand how the earth could fail them. But it had failed them, and there they were waiting in another summer for an autumn harvest that would never come."[2] Such a response as Caldwell's was grounded in essentially economic concerns and was a response to a South that was real and could not be ignored.

I believe that this body of social criticism was and is an indispensable part of the Southern renascence, that some of the greatest figures of the renascence participated, at least partly, in it, and that it must be weighted in the balances when we are defining the character of the remarkable literary resurgence that the South has known.

I should like to look briefly at some works by four writers of fiction who were committed in varying ways to such social criticism of sections of the South once notorious for their poor whites. These writers are T. S. Stribling, Thomas Wolfe, Erskine Caldwell, and Flannery O'Connor.

At first glance, these writers may seem to be strangely grouped. Thomas Wolfe, an early apostle of James Joyce and a writer of *Bildungsromans,* would apparently not belong in such a group at all. Flannery O'Connor, with her deep involvement with theological issues within the framework of Catholic belief, seemed to have different objectives from those of the others. I am not intending to suggest that these four writers, each of them in his way representative of fairly widespread movements, did have a great deal in common except a concern with a common subject matter and an attitude that reflected a basic sense of deprivation in the lives of their characters. Certainly they wrote for different audiences, from different points of view, and for different motives. They shared, however, an interest in the twentieth-century Piedmont and mountain South and its people and their problems.

T. S. Stribling was an obvious disciple of Sinclair Lewis. In 1922 he published his first significant novel, *Birthright,* which is concerned with the hopeless struggle of an educated mulatto to return to a Tennessee town, and make his way in a world dominated by prejudice, narrow-mindedness, and misunderstandings at every point. The attack upon the small town by the Lewisian method is everywhere manifest in *Birthright.* In 1926, in *Teeftallow,* Stribling produced a bitterly realistic novel of a Tennessee mountain town, emphasizing its bigotry, its ignorance, its pietistic hypocrisy, and its crushing of those who do not conform. Certainly *Teeftallow* is discernably similar to *Main Street* in subject and tone. It also draws a telling picture of a Southern small town politician, Railroad Jones, who builds his way into dominance in the town and into riches for himself, all of this resting upon his playing upon the cupidity of his townsmen. In 1928 again Stribling attempted to penetrate the nature of the pietistically religious, superstitious, small towns in their crassness, ugliness, materialism, and narrow suspicion of those from outside, in *Bright Metal,* the story of a sophisticated woman's marriage into a Tennessee mountain town and her adjustment to this environment. Stribling's major work came in the early thirties. It is a trilogy, *The Forge* (1931), *The Store* (1932), and *Unfinished Cathedral* (1934), dealing with the middle-class Vaiden family in and around Florence, Alabama, its rise from its near poor-white status to its dominance as an important family in the region, its collapse after the Civil War into the poor-white class, the building of a fortune by Miltiades Vaiden, former leader of the Ku Klux Klan, who attempts by various means and ultimately by a major and unscrupulous theft to build a store upon which his fortune shall rest, and who finally, in the last novel of the trilogy, set in the days of Muscle Shoals, has achieved his local greatness, and tries to build a cathedral to be his monument to the future. He has a quadroon sister, who is the mother of his son for whose death he is responsible. He has a daughter whose liaison with a local boy during an attempted lynching results in her subsequent marriage to a schoolteacher attracted by her obvious charms. These books are realistic studies in a broadly satiric manner of the conditions of Southern life, and they bring under continuous scrutiny the ideal of an aristocratic South and subject it to iconoclastic examination. The result is a picture of middle-class and poor-white life existing just above the level of poverty. Stribling's portrait of the South is devastating, and it is little wonder that the Agrarians turned upon him in rage and called him a "scalawag" writer. Donald Davidson, for example, in reviewing *Teeftallow* called it "the sort of realism that turns up stones in Tennessee pastures in order to display the slime and the crawling, hideous creatures underneath."[3]

Stribling's novels are seldom marked by a very high level of literary accomplishment. He writes with a crude and blunt directness, destroys his sometimes fascinating characters by making them more often the instruments of his satire than the subjects of his art, and has a certain juvenile quality that undercuts his obvious seriousness. There is no reason to revive his novels, although anyone seriously interested in the totality of literary experience in the South in the twentieth century can ignore *The Forge, The Store,* and *Unfinished Cathedral* only at the risk at being ignorant of many of the sources of far better works which came later. The significance of Stribling is that he recognized the subject matter of the middle-class and poor-white South existing in the Piedmont and mountain sections, and that he wrote a series of novels treating this material seriously as a commentary on one Southern way of life. In so doing, he established a manner and he fore-shadowed with remarkable accuracy a great many of the themes which later were to be undertaken by better writers. Without intending to suggest for one moment that William Faulkner borrowed the energy, the art, or even the plots of his works from anyone other than his own private daemon, I think that it is worthy of note that Faulkner did purchase upon publication and preserve until his death copies of Strib-ling's trilogy,[4] and that the history of the Vaidens, their decline to the level of the shiftless white, and their rise through unscrupulous methods to the control of the bank and then the town parallels closely enough the saga of the Snopes clan and the history and the treatment of miscegenation parallel *Absalom, Absalom!* closely enough to suggest that in walking Frenchman's Bend and Sutpen's Hundred Faulkner was follow-ing at however much higher a level of excellence the footsteps of an early trail blazer. It is Stribling as trail blazer upon whom I would center your attention. He discovered a lode of subject matter in the South and a method for mining that lode, and the example of his limited success in dealing with it must be measured against the far greater success of others who mined with higher skill the lodes which he had initially pointed out.

While Stribling was producing this work, Edith Summers Kelley in 1922 wrote *Weeds,* a grimly realistic picture of the life of the sharecropper's wife in Kentucky. *Weeds,* a book that deserves far broader circulation than it has received in recent years, establishes, too, a pattern which was to be followed for a long time and which added an edge of bitterness and willingness to discuss the ugly facts of life to the concern with "plain people" which Ellen Glasgow had been showing in her novels since the turn of the century.

Thomas Wolfe's South was the mountain world which, with only slight changes, Stribling had portrayed in *Bright Metal* and *Teeftallow*. Certainly his subject was primarily his own individual growth and his struggle toward identity. Yet it was a growth and a struggle that took place against a definite and sharply realized place. Even in his *Bildungsroman, Look Homeward, Angel* the people, customs, and beliefs of his home town are drawn in depth and with unflattering attention to warts and weaknesses. He declared that he had begun writing under the influence of James Joyce and that he had first written a lyric mode. He came at last to seek "objectivity" and to attempt the portrayal of an outer world.[5] That world was often New York and Europe, but it was also—until the end—the South of middle-class small towns and cities, and upon it he turned a distinctly satiric touch. In *You Can't Go Home Again,* which is more nearly a collection of short novels and sketches than a unified work, three instances might be cited: "I Have a Thing to Tell You," a short novel attacking the German Third Reich and written with almost startling objectivity; "The House That Jack Built," a short novel describing through satiric portrait and recurrent symbol the injustice and insecurity of the rich in New York; and the last five chapters of Book One of the novel, much of which was originally written as a short novel "Boom Town," and portions of which were published in *The American Mercury* and the *New Masses.*[6] In all these sections Wolfe writes with directness, impersonality, and in a style which, when compared to most of his work, is barren. Few more devastating attacks on crass materialism, impersonal capitalism, and surrender of moral values in a Southern town have been drawn than those in the "Boom Town" section. It is Stribling's attitude presented by a novelist of great merit, much as Faulkner's Snopeses are Stribling's poor-whites portrayed by a genius.

Thus Wolfe came back at the end of his life to a position which he had held as early as 1923 when he had written contemptuously of "people who shout 'Progress, Progress, Progress'—when what they mean is more Ford automobiles, more Rotary Clubs, more Baptist Ladies Social Unions.... What I shall try to get into their dusty, little pint-measure minds is that a full belly, a good automobile does not make them one whit better or finer,—that there is beauty in this world,—beauty even in this wilderness of ugliness and provincialism."[7] Now that is the brashness of youth mixed with the brashness of Lewis, but there is every reason to believe that Wolfe never deserted the position or changed his belief that it was a defensible—even a fine—subject for fictional treatment. Yet few writers have been more intensely of the South or—whatever you may think of the problem of form—are more essential to the Southern renascence. One of the Agrarians once suggested that Wolfe went to the wrong college; I think he is wrong, for Wolfe was simply true to the impulse he felt to love and write of his region while subjecting it to serious criticism.

And I think that, at least in the beginning, this was also true of Erskine Caldwell. In his autobiography Caldwell says of *Tobacco Road:* "I felt that I would never be able to write successfully about other people in other places until first I had written the story of the landless and poverty-stricken families living on East Georgia sand hills and tobacco roads. . . . I wanted to tell the story of the people I knew in the manner in which they actually lived their lives . . . and to tell it without regard for fashions in writing and traditional plots. It seemed to me that the most authentic and enduring materials of fiction were the people themselves."[8] In *Tobacco Road* Caldwell wrote with great simplicity and force of style—a clean, hard, clear, and forceful prose—of the lives of people so stripped of economic and social hope that they become grotesques and parodies of human beings, twisted by the simplest hungers and lacking in dignity or integrity. The stage version has produced the view that this story is comic. Caldwell has expressed his distress at this view and has suggested that the desire to portray, the desire to define, and a substantial degree of social anger are behind his early efforts. "All I wanted to do," he has said, "was simply to describe to the best of my ability the aspirations and despair of the people I wrote about."[9]

He was to continue describing the people of his depleted South in many novels and stories. At least two other novels and a number of his short stories demand our consideration when we write of the renascence. *God's Little Acre* follows the people of the depleted countryside to a cotton mill village during a strike. *Trouble in July* is a powerful lynching novel. Perhaps the finest single piece of work of Caldwell's is the short novel "Kneel to the Rising Sun," a story of a sadistic white land-owner, a spineless tenant farmer, and a courageous but doomed Negro. Those who think of Caldwell exclusively in terms of the semi-pornographic paperbacks which in recent years have made him one of the best-selling novelists of all time, might well re-read this grim tale of wanton cruelty, injustice, and cowardice. It has a controlled fury that lingers in the mind and heart, and it is written with an apparently artless simplicity which the artist can achieve only after many hours of seeking for clarity and grace.

Flannery O'Connor has taken what are essentially these same people and almost this same locale and has fashioned from them, their lives, and their frustrations a series of short stories and two novels rich in religious symbolisms that speak to the present world with great authority. Her characters and Caldwell's are remarkably similar and one has the feeling that they might move with relative ease from the books of one writer to the other and be at home. That this similarity is present should not be surprising, for both writers are dealing with the same region and its poor-whites and Negroes, people to whom sex and religion are practically the only interludes in a world of ignorance and despair. The characters of each writer are truly grotesques—that is, distorted or twisted permanently out of the normal. I think that *A Good Man Is Hard To Find,* Miss O'Connor's first collection of short stories, is her best work—although her total production assays remarkably high—and of that group of tales, I think the best is the final short novel, "The Displaced Person." There is not a character in "The Displaced Person" who would have trouble orienting himself in *God's Little Acre.* Yet there is a tremendous difference between the approaches of Erskine Caldwell and Flannery O'Connor to their worlds.

Caldwell's people are twisted and misshapen by social and economic deprivation. Fertilize the soil, return the price of cotton to a subsistence level, supply them with opportunity, and hope will follow and in another generation something like the good life may return. It is the system that is wrong, and the system is remediable. Hence, the social anger and the protest.

Not so with Flannery O'Connor. For her these people are made grotesque by their unsatisfied hunger for God, and around them she weaves her religious, almost theological themes. The twisted lives which Erskine Caldwell saw and drew become in her hands telling metaphors for the restless soul's disquiet when it rejects the God it seeks. But the materials she uses are indigenous to her time and place. If the peacocks in "The Displaced Person" are epiphanies of God's love for man, they are also like the fowls that roosted in the trees around the O'Connor farmhouse outside Milledgeville. If Mr. Guizac, the displaced person, brings salvation to Mrs. McIntyre's farm, he does it by displaying the virtues of neatness, cleanliness, and mechanic skill, and we must wait for Mrs. McIntyre to say, "Christ was just another D.P."[10] before we can be certain that Miss O'Connor intends us to see this story as a parable of the rejection of Christ.

Miss O'Connor's succinct, witty, and very direct style is a far cry from Stribling's overwritten sentences or Wolfe's rhetoric, but it is applied with great success to picturing her segment of the South as a microcosm of the human lot. Like Hawthorne, Miss O'Connor wanted to produce a work which had physical substance enough to stand alone and yet bodied forth some deep philosophic truth. Her truth was Catholic and universal, but her physical substance was distinctively Southern and clearly related to a part of the South which was far removed from the historical heritage of aristocratic grace and chivalric dignity and honor.

I have tried to suggest that there is a body of Southern material represented by Stribling, Wolfe, Caldwell, and O'Connor which is close to the tradition of social realism rather than that of the Joycean aesthetics or the *Kunstlerroman*. Lest you should have to take such a view on faith, I should like to suggest that it can be tested by a reading of Book One of *You Can't Go Home Again* as a portrayal of middle-class materialism in the manner of Sinclair Lewis; "Kneel to the Rising Sun," as a portrayal of hopelessness created by extreme poverty; and "The Displaced Person," as a portrayal of spiritual deprivation and denial. These works have certain characteristics in common which are worth noting. In the first place, none of these stories is centered in the individual or the individual's growth or development. Each describes a social world outside the narrator and places its emphasis on the conduct of people in that social world. In other words, each belongs, in its differing way, to the broad school of social fiction.

In the second place—and this is true even of the selection by Wolfe—the styles are remarkably uniform, not mixed;[11] that is, each writer in these selections maintains a single voice. Wolfe's is literary, edging toward rhetoric, but essentially geared to the satiric presentation of a slightly exaggerated transcript from life. Caldwell's is simple, direct, with underlying folk rhythms, resulting in part from repetition and in part from a folk vocabulary. Miss O'Connor's is clear, sharply focused, simple, sardonic and detached in tone but possessed of great energy.

In the third place, all deal with distinctively Southern subject matter, but with people and places outside the setting of the Tidewater or the Deep South, and with characters who can accurately be called grotesque. Wolfe wrote scathingly of the ugliness of the life of the hill people—what he called the "mountain grills"—and certainly blind and syphilitic Judge Rumford Bland should rank high on any list of grotesques. Yet the characters of these three writers are really less literary grotesques than non-Southern critics would have us believe. These authors have not made grotesques: they have pictured tormented, twisted, and diseased lives which most of us can recognize as actually existing and within our experience. As Miss O'Connor once said, "Any fiction that comes out of the South is going to be called grotesque by northern readers— unless it is really grotesque. Then—it is going to be called photographic realism."[12]

A fourth common characteristic that these works share is a consistent vision of the unrealized potential in the life of the section they describe. All of these works portray characters defeated and depleted by social forces and circumstances that impoverish their lives. Wolfe's characters are the victims of a false sense of values in a business world. Caldwell's are the victims of grinding economic depression. Miss O'Connor's are the victims of a religious environment that stifles the hunger for God. All, too, are looking forward, not backward, outward not inward, and each in his own way is preaching change.

Yes, I think we must insist that social criticism was a legitimate and significant part of the Southern renascence. But the social conditions which called this wave of criticism forth are passing or have passed. Caldwell's characters' children have moved to town and they buy a new car every two or three years and their children are in high school and applying for fellowships to the University of Georgia. Wolfe's characters batten on affluence and their towns are now cities. Miss O'Connor's people are closer to our time, and, significantly, their problem is really not economic poverty.

The moment when Mr. Tate's backward look was fruitful has passed. The history it embraced is recognized as legend and manipulated as myth and it has lost its generative force. Is the same thing also true of the social criticism of the renascence? As tobacco roads give way to interstate highways, as country stores become shopping centers, as small towns become the suburban areas of booming cities, is the South as social subject any longer relevant? Can one take the glass-enclosed elevator to the twenty-second floor of the Regency-Hyatt in Atlanta and look out upon a world distinctively different from what he might see in New York, Chicago, or Los Angeles, even if he doesn't glance at the nationally televised game being played in the Falcons' and Braves' splendid new stadium, or listen to the homogenized accents of its announcer? The answer is that he can, if he looks closely enough at home. As Louis Rubin pointed out to me, within two blocks of the Regency-Hyatt you can find street evangelists extolling their primitive religions in tone and manner that make you think Hazel Motes of *Wise Blood* has come back to life.

Now certainly the problems have changed, but I believe that the characteristics that distinguish the region from the rest of the nation are still distinctively here, and that they give a special Southern aspect and a unique value to the artistic representation of life in the United States. These distinctive characteristics are, as you may recall that I asserted in the beginning, the presence of the Negro and the shame of his enslavement and second-class citizenship; the historical experience of military defeat, military occupation, and reconstruction; and a predominantly agricultural economy. Only one of these—the agricultural economy—seems likely to pass soon; and to the extent to which the Southern renascence assumed such an agrarian way of life, that renascence ended with the Second World War. But the South remains a self-conscious region. Its hamlets may become towns, its towns cities; its accent may be flattened by television and radio; its passion for religious dimensions to life may take the form of studied ritual rather than primitive spontaneity; but so long as the Negro remains and the history can speak with authority, the South will be a potent subject for serious art. That art will, I believe, continue to be interested both in the problems of social situations and in those of individual development and identity. I hope, and believe, that Southern writers will continue to use these problems with high seriousness and great relevancy. After all, as Miss O'Connor once observed, "Southern writers are stuck with the South, and it's a very good thing to be stuck with."[13]

NOTES

1. "The New Provincialism," *Collected Essays* (Denver, 1959), pp. 292–293.
2. "After Ten Years" [Introduction], *Tobacco Road,* Modern Library Ed., (New York, 1940), pp. [viii–ix].
3. "T. S. Stribling, Critic's Almanac, April 18, 1926," in *The Spyglass: Views and Reviews, 1924–1930,* ed. John T. Fain (Nashville, Tenn., 1963), pp. 13–14.
4. Joseph Blotner, *William Faulkner's Library—A Catalogue* (Charlottesville, Va., 1964), p. 54.
5. *The Letters of Thomas Wolfe,* ed. Elizabeth Nowell (New York, 1956), p. 700.
6. "Boom Town" in the May, 1934, *American Mercury,* and "The Company," in the January 11, 1938, *New Masses.*
7. *The Letters of Thomas Wolfe to His Mother,* ed. C. Hugh Holman and Sue Fields Ross (Chapel Hill, N. C., 1968), p. 42.
8. *Call It Experience* (New York, 1951), pp. 101–102.
9. *Ibid.,* p. 132.
10. *A Good Man Is Hard to Find and Other Stories* (New York, 1955), p. 243.
11. See Leonard Lutwack, "Mixed and Uniform Prose Styles in the Novel," in *The Theory of the Novel,* ed. Philip Stevick (New York, 1967), pp. 209–219.
12. "A Collection of Statements," in *The Added Dimension: The Art and Mind of Flannery O'Conner,* ed. Melvin J. Friedman and Lewis A. Lawson (New York, 1966), p. 243.
13. *Ibid.,* p. 239.

Second Thoughts on the Old Gray Mare:
THE CONTINUING RELEVANCE OF SOUTHERN LITERARY ISSUES
LOUIS D. RUBIN, JR.

WHEN WE PRESUME to talk about the South, and what the future may hold for its writers, we ought first to ask ourselves what it is that we wish to know, and why we wish to know it. Novelists themselves seldom ponder such questions; I doubt for example that William Faulkner ever spent much time consciously brooding over the present and future of Southern writing. Indeed, many Southern writers are actively uninterested in being known as Southern writers; they go to some lengths to deny that they are anything known as a "Southern writer." And one can understand why. No good writer likes the notion of provincialism and limitation implied thereby; he doesn't care to think of himself grouped along with John Trotwood Moore, Augusta Evans Wilson, and Harry Stillwell Edwards as exemplars of the literary genius of Dixie. And he doesn't like the implied chauvinism, the lingering aura of the United Daughters of the Confederacy literary tradition, whereby mediocre poets and shallow storytellers are pridefully extolled because they are Ours. To the extent, therefore, that the question of whether the Southern renascence will continue into the future notably involves motives of sectional patriotism, so does it seem not merely distasteful but indeed

dangerous to good critics and readers as well. We who theorize about Southern literature ought constantly to bear that
difficulty in mind. To what extent are we, in however erudite
and scholarly a fashion, engaged in waving the Confederate
flag when we talk about writers as Southerners? Are we, if
less naively and ingenuously perhaps than our predecessors,
nevertheless engaged in composing our contemporary version
of that once-desired non-partisan history of The War Between
the States written from the Southern point of view?

The difficulty we face in this respect is that, as Southern
readers and critics, we read and we think out of a tradition
that for many years was strongly patriotic, based on deep
sectional needs and regional loyalties that arose out of what
were not literary so much as political and social conditions.
The demand for a Southern literature, as distinct from an
American literature, first made itself felt during the decades
preceding the Civil War, when the South was engaged in
insisting on its own separate political identity. There is all too
much truth to the jest that when the Southern States met in
convention in Nashville in 1850 to discuss sectional needs and
tactics, resolutions were passed to the effect that *"Resolved:*
that there be established a Southern Literature. *Resolved:* that
the Honorable William Gilmore Simms be requested to write
it."* Afterward, in the years following the War, when the local
color movement was at its height and Southern writers seemed
to some critics to dominate the American literary scene,
considerable patriotism was mixed into the motives both of
the writers themselves and the Southern critics who wrote so
pridefully about them. And when the vogue of local color
passed, and Southern letters receded into a state so comatose
and feeble-blooded as to elicit H. L. Mencken's famous indict-
ment in "The Sahara of the Bozart," much of the criticism
written by Southerners about Southern writers was pathetically
chauvinistic and insular, seeking to convince a dubious world
that shallowness was admirable because it was Southern. You
will find the sentiment entombed in so many of the bio-

graphical sketches introducing the work of now-forgotten Southern poetasters and sentimentalists in that vast compendium of patriotic mediocrity, *The Library of Southern Literature*. Little wonder, then, that in 1923, when *Poetry* magazine called upon Southern poets to "accept the challenge of a region so specialized in beauty, so rich in racial tang and prejudice, so jewel-weighted with a heroic past,"[1] the Nashville Fugitives strongly dissented, with Allen Tate declaring that "we fear very much to have the slightest stress laid upon Southern traditions in literature; we who are Southerners know the fatality of such an attitude—the old atavism and sentimentality are always imminent. . . ."[2]

The question might have been permitted to recede into the past, along with the ageing veterans of the onetime Confederacy, had it not been that not only those Fugitives of Nashville but a host of other Southerners as well began publishing, in the late 1920s and in the 1930s and thereafter, literature of such signal accomplishment and importance that it became impossible to ignore considerations of time and place when dealing with it. In the year 1929 alone, for example, Faulkner published *Sartoris* and *The Sound and the Fury*, Wolfe *Look Homeward, Angel*, Cabell *The Way of Ecben*, Glasgow *They Stooped to Folly*, Heyward *Mamba's Daughters*, Merrill Moore *The Noise That Time Makes*, Tate his biography of Jefferson Davis, Warren his biography of John Brown, and Erskine Caldwell his first collection of short stories. The roster of important Southern writers between the two world wars, including not only those just mentioned but Ransom, Davidson, Porter, Welty, McCullers, Green, Lytle, Roberts, Stribling, Hellman, Gordon, Bishop, Brooks, and others, was such as to make critics and readers everywhere conscious not only of their existence but of their regional identity. For clearly there *was* a common identity; there were certain recognizable characteristics to their work, traits, interests and attitudes that all of them seemed to share, none of them peculiarly Southern perhaps but, taken in the aggregate and in their recurrent presence within the novels, stories, and poems, more than enough to make people talk and think about a distinctly *Southern* kind of writing.

Precisely what is this Southern quality, or qualities, that characterizes its writings has been a matter of some dispute. For Allen Tate it is "a literature conscious of the past in the present."[3] For Robert B. Heilman it is "the coincidence of a sense of the concrete, a sense of the elemental, a sense of the ornamental, a sense of the representative, and a sense of totality."[4] Frederick J. Hoffman believes it has to do with a literature of "place," with all the historical, cultural, and social factors thereto appended.[5] I prefer to think of it as at bottom an attitude toward the nature of man in society that can best be described by the word "religious"—though, I hasten to add, by no means sectarian. But whatever the quality, this much seemed undeniable: the South, as it was and it is, was deeply involved in the work of these writers. When so many good writers appeared within the matter of a decade or so, while in the decades before them so little important literature had been produced by Southerners, and when so much of their work had an identifiable and recognizable shared quality, mere coincidence could not be a sufficient explanation. Something about the bounded geographic region in which they were born, and about the specific history and culture of that region, must of necessity be involved.

To come to grips with this body of literature, however, which of itself no longer demanded any impulse involving chauvinism, the Southern critic has labored under a long heritage of flag-waving—Southern literature for the sake of Southern pride—and an equally long heritage of conscious political sectionalism—Southern literature as the antithesis of, and existing in contrast to, "Northern" literature. And for the Southern critic the job has been to divest himself of this excess historical baggage, in order to deal with literature which not only stands in no need of sectionalism in order for its excellence to be appreciated, but which demands for its proper understanding a disinterested criticism which can identify and evaluate for what it is the impulse toward sectionalism that has been so important a feature of Southern life and is therefore embodied in the literature.

And yet, having said that, one must at once enter a demurrer to the effect that not only are novelists intensely human, but so are literary critics, and it would be useless to pretend that there are not mixed in within the complexity of motives that lead men to write novels, and lead other men to read and to criticize them, just such impulses toward sectional identification and assertion. In few of the Southern writers, perhaps, did the desire for regional identity reach the level of conscious statement that it did for the Agrarians of Nashville, but in one form or the other it was and still is present among them all. So that among the equipment which the Southern critic can bring to the task of analyzing and understanding Southern literature, sectional identity and sectional pride are not to be despised. It is not, for example, merely the critical intelligence of a Cleanth Brooks that makes his study of the novels of William Faulkner the best guide to the accomplishment of that writer; it is also his intense emotional engagement with the novels and with the region. Brooks' pride in Faulkner, tempered as it is by an acute critical intelligence and a shaping imagination, plays no insignificant part in his critical success. Not, therefore, the denial of the complex factors of identification and pride, but the disciplined harnessing of such impulses, so that they do not dominate but are placed at the service of the intelligence and the understanding, is what is needed. When, to choose another example, Hugh Holman so masterfully interprets Thomas Wolfe in terms of the particular characteristics of Wolfe's Piedmont Southern heritage, he is able to do so not because he denies that he too is a product of the Piedmont South, but because he is able to recognize, in himself and therefore in Wolfe, just what that heritage has made possible.

I have gone into what might seem to be this long digression into the past and present problems of the critic of Southern literature because we cannot make much sense of the problem we address ourselves to today unless we realize the extent to which, merely by phrasing the question in the way we have done, we are involved in its answer. Will the Southern renascence continue into future generations? To make any kind of meaningful answer, we must decide not only what the question means, but why it is asked.

We ask it, I think, not merely because as readers and as critics we are curious as to whether an interesting phenomenon will continue to exist. More than mere curiosity is involved. Most of us who have admired the work of the Southern writers of the last quarter-century and more would *like* for it to continue. We would like for the South to continue to be one of the leading forces in the literature of our country, and we have been gratified at its having been so. There are certain issues on which our region has not shown up to very good advantage. The South has been caught up in a process of transition which has been marked by considerable turmoil and ugliness. Its literature has been one of the happier products of this process. Not merely along with, but indeed *directly out of* the turmoil and even the violence of the changing South, there have come novels and poems which not only have fixed the image of the South in art, but have given to it the imaginative dignity of tragedy and comedy. In particular William Faulkner has created high tragedy out of the Southern experience. Not only does this afford Southerners the occasion for much understandable pride, but it also constitutes assurance that what has been going on in the region during Faulkner's and our lifetimes is not simply ugly, but also highly meaningful, so that the confused positions we have occupied add up finally to a drama of definition, with the contending forces representing not merely sordid self-interest but profoundly important human needs and aspirations.

Previously I suggested that I thought that the distinguishing characteristic of the literature of the modern South was its essentially religious nature. I mean by this that the image of human life that it represents is one in which the values embodied in it—love and honor and pity and pride and compassion and sacrifice, to adopt Faulkner's memorable assessment—have not been relativistic, arbitrary, materialistic, but absolute, unswerving, spiritual. Its human confrontations have not been the clash of ignorant armies by night, but the high drama of the soul. The Southern writer has habitually seen man as by nature a creature of society, and has seen his alienation from society as tragic, and he has also depicted the base of human action as essentially moral. He has seldom ascribed the test of his behavior as one of social efficacy alone. In the novels of Faulkner and his fellow Southern writers, what men do and think *matters,* and this has given to the characters a dignity and importance that transcends the merely biological and economic.

With this attitude toward human experience has gone a number of literary characteristics, some of which might at first glance appear to be purely formal in nature, but all of which ultimately depend for their validity upon that attitude. The historical sense, the assumption that what human beings have done in time is meaningful and that men are creatures of time and are molded by what has transpired before them, rests absolutely upon the conviction of the importance of what men can achieve; for if human life ultimately means nothing, and if there are no values which transcend the requirements of the moment, then the past is indeed a bucket of ashes, and only what *is,* and not how it came to be or what it may some day turn out to be, is of any interest.

Not only Robert Heilman but numerous other critics have recognized in Southern literature a devotion to the concrete, the specific, along with a distrust of the abstract. It has been the rich texture of the Southern novel and the Southern poem as well, "things as they are in their rich and contingent materiality,"[6] as Ransom put it, that has given body and form to the artistic image. The sodden greys, the drab surfaces of the naturalistic novelists, for example, have found little coun-

39

terpart in Southern writing, for the reason that the Southern writer has characteristically been unwilling and unable to subordinate the complexity of human life in time and place to the demands of any ruling thesis or theory that would oversimplify or unduly limit his experience. Systems, theories, dialectics tend to reduce the complexity and variety of human response, in that they would isolate certain factors and attempt to judge and interpret the actions and experience of men in terms of those factors alone. Just as men resist the impoverishment of such systematizing, so the Southern writer has insisted upon complexity, and has habitually delighted in the particular, the concrete, even the eccentric. The well-known Southern addiction to rhetoric, for the full resources of language in its connotative as well as denotative potentialities, is grounded in this passion for specificity of detail; the Southern writer's addiction to the high style of discourse, his susceptibility to excess of diction, is a natural consequence both of his traditional belief in the complexity of experience, and of his willingness to invoke moral and ethical values in order to define and judge the experience of men. Rhetoric becomes ludicrous the instant we cease to sympathize with it; it depends upon the ultimate importance we are willing to give to what men say and feel, and to the individuality of their own particular ways of expressing it. The language of *Absalom, Absalom!* would seem empty and meaningless if Faulkner did not believe that what Thomas Sutpen did and sought was *important,* and if he did not make us think so too.

Thus when we find ourselves asking whether the South will continue to produce important fiction, it is in part a question of whether the meaning that the writers of the Southern renascence have given to our experience will remain applicable and whether the moral and ethical values that they have ascribed to human experience will continue to be valid. Inherent in the literature of Faulkner, Wolfe, Warren and the others is a judgment of the nature and the importance of human life in time and place, and in particular of our lives in our time and place.

We do not like to think this estimate of human potentiality is inadequate and outdated, and so not surprisingly, we find ourselves examining the work of the writers of the generation following that of Faulkner, Wolfe, and the other writers of the 1920s and 1930s, to see whether there has been a slackening, a falling off in quality. Has the Southern renascence run its course, and is the remarkable upsurge in the creative vitality of a region that began manifesting itself after the first world war a thing of the past, with the yield steadily dwindling as the South advances further and further into the second half of the twentieth century? And if so, what does this mean about the Southern experience of our own day?

For many of us, the problem has involved something of a dilemma. On the one hand, we have fervently desired a change in some of the South's most traditional attitudes. In particular the place of the Negro in the South has seemed to us to merit considerable revision. The inhumanity and injustice of the South's treatment of the Negro have weighed heavily upon the Southern conscience. Yet paradoxically, the presence of the Negro in the South, and the position he has occupied in the South, have been closely associated with a kind of rural society, and an attitude toward the nature of man in society and the human values by which we seek to order our lives, that we are loth to surrender, and which the literature of the South has distinctively embodied. We face, therefore, the prospect of seeing the Negro accorded the full and unrestricted participation in our society that he merits as part of the change of that society to one that is predominately urban and industrial—one in which many of the aspects of Southern life that we have admired and cherished seem to be threatened with imminent extinction. And if this is what is happening, then it would seem to follow that a literary mode based upon that kind of society and embodying its values and beliefs will likewise become obsolete and outdated.

All this, therefore, is implied in the question of whether the so-called Southern literary renascence is over. Consequently, when we read the fiction of Styron and O'Connor and others of the post-World War II Southern writers to see whether the creativity of the Southern literary imagination remains alive and unimpaired, our curiosity is more than merely that of literary historians. What we are asking is, can a region which has been changing—and in certain important ways changing to better advantage—continue to afford its writers, and by extension ourselves as well, the quality of human definition in time, and the attitude toward human potentiality and limitation, that in the past it has managed so well?

It is in this light that I interpret the almost uniformly favorable reaction of Southern critics and reviewers to the recent publication of William Styron's novel *The Confessions of Nat Turner*. For here was a novel by a leading post-World War II Southern writer of fiction, which was clearly and undeniably constructed and told in the old Southern tragic mode, with all the familiar attributes—the rhetorical high style, the strong man engaged in a struggle against time, the religious attitude toward human experience on both the protagonist's part and the author's, the complexity of a dense social texture, the individual seen as irretrievably a man in society, yet possessed of his own solitude and capable of the exercise of his own free will. Yet there was one telling difference between this novel and those of Styron's great predecessors. He told his story not merely from the point of view of the Negro slave Nat Turner, but in so doing he assumed the Negro slave to be fully human, capable of every moral impulse and every complex thought that a white man could know, so that the only difference existing between Nat Turner and any white man was what society had decreed. In other words, it was the first major Southern novel in which a Negro protagonist was depicted as a fully equal individual, the first "integrated" Southern novel, so to speak. Thus Styron had at once continued the best of the old human values of the Southern novel, and yet on the quintessential Southern political and social question had written his book squarely out of the attitudes

42

of the enlightened contemporary urban South. It was hardly surprising, then, that book reviewers and critics throughout the South received his work with a tremendous sense of satisfaction; for what Styron had in effect told them was, See, it can still be done, just as before; we can combine the best of our old way with the best of the new way, so that we need not give up the human values of the Southern community in order to live in the modern world.

Perhaps I overrate *The Confessions of Nat Turner,* and if so it is doubtless for precisely those reasons, but to me it is a major work of fiction, and demonstrates conclusively what I have long contended, which is that the South's potentiality for continuing to nurture important literature is still far from exhausted, and that if indeed the cultural conditions which made possible the literature of the generation of Faulkner and Wolfe are fated to disappear as the South urbanizes, it will take a great deal more urbanizing than has thus far occurred. Of course I am aware that it is possible to point to significant differences between Styron's art and that of his predecessors, but it seems to me that the similarities are still fully as important as the differences, and that the differences represent the necessary accommodations of a succeeding generation's attitudes to the facts of its own experience—an experience that in some important respects remains essentially continuous.

Yet I face, in that assertion, the argument to the contrary, advanced some thirty years ago by Allen Tate, and developed with so much insight and persuasiveness by Walter Sullivan.[7] The argument is that as the South has changed from one kind of society into another—and the words rural and urban are perhaps only the best possible approximations for what the change has been—the breakdown of the moral and ethical social structure that was the Old South has advanced to such an extent that the so-called "historical dimension," the contrast between the religious and social order that the Old South made available as an image for its writers, and the secular, materialistic mass society of modern America that is now our experience, is no longer possible. Thus the collapse of the old order that was going on throughout the western world in the nineteenth and early twentieth centuries, which permitted to the artist the momentary individual solution and the undeniable artistic achievement of the so-called "novel of growth" wherein the old absolutes of religion, nationalism, and ethical progress were supplanted by the new divinity of art, took the form, in the early twentieth-century South, of the collapse of a myth, the myth of the "Old South." Now that the myth no longer can be taken sufficiently seriously to make possible even the meaningful rejection of it, the particular focus of consciousness, the meeting of past and present, the "looking two ways"[8] as Tate has termed it, can no longer give to the writer's work the important image of particularity that made possible the Southern renascence.

This is a very formidable argument. In one sense there is no way to refute it. But let us recognize it for what it is. It is not in essence a literary argument. It is a cultural, perhaps even a religious argument, and one that I associate, in its non-Southern manifestations, with T. S. Eliot, Oswald Spengler, Henry Adams, and with that host of profound thinkers who view the events of the past six or seven hundred years as representing a "Decline of the West," the breakdown of civilization and culture as western man has known them, the recrudescence of a new age of barbarism attendant upon the collapse of Christianity. In the nineteenth century Matthew Arnold stated the premises about as well as anyone in "Dover Beach": "The Sea of Faith/Was once too at the full, and round earth's shore/Lay like the folds of a bright girdle furled./But now I only hear/Its melancholy, long, withdrawing roar. . . ." Surely there are times when the most optimistic among us feel like that; and if Matthew Arnold could experience such a devastation because of the London dock strikes, what must we feel, when each morning's newspaper and each evening's television newscast bring the tidings they have been bringing us these last several decades?

Do not think that I exaggerate when I say that the "decline and fall of the myth of the Old South" argument is part and parcel of that general cultural position about the collapse of western Christian society. The assumptions are precisely the same. I quote Mr. Sullivan himself, from an extremely fine essay of some fifteen years ago about the Civil War in Southern fiction:

> . . . . in the Old South the honor and the pride were there, not as individual virtues in isolated men, but as a part of the public consciousness, the moral basis on which the culture was constructed. That is the reason that the War has been used so often by so many Southern writers. It is the grand image for the novelist, the period when the "ultimate truths," with which Mr. Faulkner says the writer must deal, existed as commonly recognized values within a social framework. It is the only moment in American history when a completely developed national ethic was brought to a dramatic crisis.[9]

Whether or not Mr. Sullivan is right in that assertion about the civilization of the Old South, this much is true: one can point to numerous passages in the work of Faulkner, Warren, Tate, and many of the other leading writers of the Southern renascence that more or less say the same thing. This much, it seems to me, is undeniable: the sense of decline and fall, of the collapsing moral order of the Old South in crass modern times, has indeed constituted a theme of striking literary efficacy for many fine Southern writers. But that this particular measuring device is by any means the only or even the most important theme or attitude that the Southern experience has afforded to its writers, I would emphatically deny. And I would also deny any real basis in actual fact to the idea, which for convenience I shall call the "decline and fall of the Old South" position. The whole argument, it seems to me, is based on a series of premises which I see no reason to take for granted, either in their general cultural assumptions or in their specific application to the question of whether a distinctively Southern, regional literary art is or is not dead.

The first premise is that the Old South furnished a superior moral ordering, however temporary, the breakdown of which provided a legitimate and actual basis for a sense of decline and fall, of a descent into crass times. I do not think that it did, and nothing that I read in Southern history makes me believe in the actual existence of any such superior moral structure in the Old South. I do not deny that many of the South's best writers have believed it did, but what they believed was a myth. And if so, then there is no reason for me to suppose that either the particular myth or others equally usable may not continue to be just as possible to the Southern writer as in the past. The notion of a "decline and fall" having taken place is an omnipresent, ever-renewable notion. One finds it throughout the correspondence of Jefferson and Adams, for example. I imagine that Charlemagne and Queen Elizabeth of England likewise felt so. The times are *always* getting worse. The past is always nobler than the present. It was in the time of the Book of Samuel, I believe, that the sister-in-law of Samuel named her son Ichabod, saying "The glory is departed from Israel."

The second premise implicit in the "decline and fall of the Old South" idea is that the qualities of imagination responsible for the excellence of so much Southern writing in the decades following the First World War were dependent for their availability upon the specific historical occasion of a South that was in the process of changing from a rural, agricultural society to an urban, industrial society. That these qualities, which I have contended are the product of an essentially religious attitude, and derive from a view of men as capable of the heroic and the tragic stature, may well have grown out of that specific historical occasion, I do not deny. But that is no reason to assume that they will not survive once the specific occasion for their having come into existence has passed. That they must and will be modified to fit a different circumstance is undeniable; but my own belief, from what I see of the region and from reading the work of not only Styron but numerous other Southern writers of a new generation, is

46

that they are so very deeply engrained within Southern experience that they will continue to assert themselves almost
indefinitely.

At bottom, I admit that this comes down to a conviction
that the religious values thereby represented remain available
because they remain valid. In other words, I do not think we
are dealing merely with literary conventions and relative
strategies; I think we are ultimately dealing with the image
of truth out of which great literature must be constructed. I
do not see those values as either verifiable by or dependent
purely upon a specific belief in the Protestant Christianity that
gave them their particular form and shape in the South; in
my belief they transcend any such sectarian origins.

The third premise that I feel goes along with the "decline
and fall" notion of Southern literature is that in changing from
a rural, agricultural to an urban, industrial society, life in the
South has changed so utterly that it no longer is, or will soon
no longer be, recognizably and identifiably Southern experience as previous generations have known it. I do not think
that is true. I am perfectly well aware that the suburbs of
Nashville physically resemble those of Detroit; but I do not
believe that all of the essential qualities of Southern life have
disappeared just because the South has become urbanized.
I do not find the human attitudes and values of life in the
South as I see it today so enormously different from what I
knew as a child growing up in a small Southern city, nor do
I find them completely different from those of the life described in the novels of writers much older than myself. An
important difference that I *do* see involves the South's attitude
toward the place of the Negro in the Southern community.
This *is* changing, and it seems to me that what is really happening is that the Negro is being brought *into* the community.
The essential community is still there. Of course there have
been changes—but there have also been important survivals.
The way that Southerners think and act and talk remains in
numerous important ways essentially unchanged. The South-

47

ern city as I see it is very much a *Southern* city, and not merely a city located in the South. So, as far as I am concerned, there has been considerable continuity along with the change, and I think that the South as a distinct place is still very much available to the writer.

The fourth and final premise I wish to note in the "decline and fall" argument is the notion that it is possible to point out a significant decline in the quality of Southern writing since the years of the renascence. I deny that any such drastic decline exists. There may be some falling off in quality, but no more than might be expected as the literary generations change. The level of attainment with such things is never uniformly constant. There are still numerous fine Southern novels being written.

I will try to be specific. I have been reading and reviewing books by Southern authors for perhaps twenty years. During that time I have seen publication of *The Golden Apples,* by Eudora Welty; *A Good Man Is Hard to Find,* by Flannery O'Connor; *A Death in the Family,* by James Agee; *The Confessions of Nat Turner* and two other fine novels by William Styron; two excellent novels by Walker Percy; and *The Sot-Weed Factor,* by John Barth, among many other books. That is a pretty good showing. Nothing I have seen has convinced me that there has been any alarming overall decline in the quality of the writing by Southerners during this period. Nor does it seem to me that these books, and many others as well, lack the abundant presence of most of the qualities we have come to associate with the literature of the modern South. The writers differ markedly among themselves, of course: like their predecessors, these writers are highly individualistic and original in their artistry. They represent, too, the experience of a newer generation, which must find its own language. To the extent that the Southern experience is changing, its writers must change with it. Yet their work remains distinctive and recognizable, the change has been taking place very much on Southern terms, and the books of Styron, Barth,

O'Connor and the other writers of the post-World War II generation constitute, in their imaginativeness and individuality, an undeniable continuation, into a new time and place, of a tradition of remarkable literary achievement.

So I cannot see any compelling reason to write off the Southern literary renascence as something which flowered brilliantly for several decades but is now finished. It may well be that the particular image of the decline and fall of the Old South that proved so useful to some of the best writers of the 1920s and 1930s has lost much of its usefulness, though I am by no means sure even of that. But this has been only one of the themes and the attitudes of modern Southern literature; it accounts for some writers but not for others, for some books but not others. It has little or nothing to do with, for example, *Look Homeward, Angel,* or *Light in August,* or *As I Lay Dying,* or *The Heart Is A Lonely Hunter,* or *A Death In The Family,* or *The Golden Apples.* These books, and many others like them, are not less distinctively of the Southern literary mode for not being based on the sense of decline and fall. And the books of the younger writers seem just as identifiably regional even though they come out of an experience that supposedly is crucially different. For one thing, novels such as Barth's *The Sot-Weed Factor* give promise of the continuation and even the intensification of what from Cabell to Faulkner to Wolfe to Welty has been an important comic inventiveness, very much a part of the Southern literary mode throughout the region's history even though not nearly so often remarked on as the literature of high tragedy. It would not be too startling to see the counterparts of Don Quixote come riding out of the Deep South and into Virginia and the Carolinas in the years ahead. Urban though it may be, the South still has a goodly quantity of its historical experience left to it. The South community has changed, but it is by no means close to extinction. Meanwhile it seems to me that neither the fear that it has gone, nor the hope that it survives, is as relevant to our purposes as the obvious fact that the region still exists, and that its writers continue to thrive. I see no reason for doubting that the continuing drama of the Southern experience is likely to remain the nurturing ground for a literature that will clearly be, in John Crowe Ransom's felicitous phrase of some years ago, "modern with the Southern accent."

NOTES

1. Harriet Monroe, "The Old South" (review of *Carolina Chansons* by DuBose Heyward and Hervey Allen), *Poetry*, XXII (May 1923), 91.
2. Letter to Marjorie Swett, dated June 22, 1923; quoted in Louise Cowan, *The Fugitive Group: A Literary History* (Baton Rouge, 1959), p. 116.
3. "The New Provincialism," *Collected Essays* (Denver, 1959), p. 292.
4. "The Southern Temper," in *Southern Renascence: The Literature of the Modern South,* ed. Louis D. Rubin, Jr., and Robert D. Jacobs (Baltimore, 1953), p. 3.
5. *The Art of Southern Fiction: A Study of Some Modern Novelists* (Carbondale, 1967), pp. 12–28.
6. "Poetry: A Note on Ontology," *The World's Body* (New York, 1938), p. 116.
7. Mr. Sullivan and I have been happily debating this matter for close to a decade now, and neither of us has succeeded remotely in convincing the other. In more morbid moments I sometimes fear that in both instances there is more than a little generalization from personal needs going on; that is, as a novelist he has been trying manfully to come to grips with the difficulties he faces in writing fiction, while as a somewhat less persistent novelist I have been desperately trying to pretend the difficulties aren't there! Of course I don't really believe this.
8. "*The Fugitive* 1922–1925: A Personal Recollection Twenty Years After," *Princeton University Library Chronicle,* III (April 1942), 83.
9. "Southern Novelists and the Civil War," in *Southern Renascence*, p. 125.

The State of Southern Fiction[1]
EDITED BY
GEORGE CORE

CORE. I think it might be good to start out with a few general remarks about the ground we have covered. Allen Tate has some things to say that have been alluded to by all three men upon occasion, and I might begin by reading two passages which are widely quoted.

> With the war of 1914–1918, the South re-entered the world—but gave a backward glance as it stepped over the border: that backward glance gave us the Southern renascence, a literature conscious of the past in the present.[2]

> From the peculiarly historical consciousness of the Southern writer has come work of a special order; but the focus of this consciousness is quite temporary. It has made possible the curious burst of intelligence we get at a crossing of the ways, not unlike, on an infinitesimal scale, the outburst of poetic genius at the end of the sixteenth century when commercial England had already begun to crush feudal England. The Histories and Tragedies of Shakespeare record the death of the old regime, and Doctor Faustus gives us feudal order for world power.[3]

Now I would like to mention a few things about Southern literature that we hope to deal with. The first one of these is that the South has always quite obviously had a sense of community, a sense of the region which has been called regionalism as opposed to provincialism. And in connection with this it has had an agricultural economy, and part of that economy has been the presence of the Negro who has been in an unequal status. The Southerner has also had a historical consciousness about his region. He has had it because the South, as Richard Weaver and Vann Woodward pointed out, is the only part of the country that has ever lost a war. And this has given him a tragic view of life, which I think is part and parcel of a religious attitude, indeed, a sacramental attitude, towards man and nature. I think Mr. Rubin made a very important point when he indicated that this is not the result of a sectarian religion. Of course it is essentially Protestant.

Another thing that we have talked about is the legend and mythology of the Old South, and Mr. Rubin has said that he doubts whether the mythology did in fact exist. But he said at the same time Southerners believed it existed, and they have been able to predicate a large body of literature upon that belief.

Another point that I would like to bring out is that the South has had a penchant for story-telling. It has an oratorical and rhetorical tradition. It has also had a sense of the concrete: the South has steered away from abstraction; and a sense of place is, of course, a part of this concreteness and is consonant with the idea of community.

Finally, I would say that the South has accomplished in its best and most characteristic literature in the renascence what Cleanth Brooks calls the "Christian synthesis," by which he means a view of life embodying the idea of history on the one hand and the sacramental attitude towards nature on the other.

I thought I would begin the discussion tonight by talking about the idea of regionalism and what it embodies and go on from there. It has struck me for a long time that good American literature, as opposed to, say, the novels of Kafka, has always been regional in the best sense. Let me ask Mr. Holman to comment on that.

Holman. I think that that is certainly true within limits, George. There developed in the early part of the nineteenth century a very self-conscious attempt on the part of the American nation to create a literature for itself. Mr. Rubin referred last night to a notorious joke about a convention in which Southern states resolved that there should be a Southern literature and that William Gilmore Simms should write it. I think that sometime during the first or second decade of the nineteenth century a fair portion of America resolved that there should be an American literature, and Washington Irving, William Cullen Bryant, and James Fenimore Cooper should write it. But, along with that particular thrust, there was at the same time a strong counter-thrust going on that realized itself in the literary wars of the forties and fifties, in which we found the New England group in particular protesting against a regional literature, and even protesting against a national literature or the attempt to write a literature definitively American. They were asking for internationalism and attempting to free literature from the bondage of jingoism and local patriotism. People like James Russell Lowell and Henry Wadsworth Longfellow were actively engaged in this movement, together with a number of others as well. At this particular time Southern writers, who were then beginning to be rather self-consciously regional because of certain social and political pressures, were also beginning to define national literature in regional terms; and almost everything, I think, that we would find said in our own time about a regional literature as the means of writing the great American novel or realizing an American fiction was said in the forties and fifties by various writers in periodicals like the *Southern Quarterly Review* and the *Southern Literary Messenger*. These journals argued the importance of creating a national literature out of a recognition of the distinctive qualities which were regional.

This attitude has changed and undergone rather complex and complicated sophistication as time has gone on. We passed through the local color movement in which it all got rather intricately involved in fantasy and sentimentality and eccentricity when, it seems to me, that what we were really talking about was not the spirit or nature or quality of life in a region but the superficial and surface eccentricities which distinguish the life in particular sections. But we have come back in the twentieth century to a very strong sense of regional literature. The South has certainly been one of the voices of that sense of regionalism, but it's not by any means unique in this. There was a very strong Midwestern literature in the latter part of the nineteenth century and in the early decades of the twentieth century and actually until around 1930. There is today a very strong far-Western literature, the literature that one of my friends calls the writing of the Pacific slope. New England has managed to remain largely aloof from such matters, but we have grown accustomed to that over the years.

Core. So writers in this country had to free themselves from England before they could become at once American and universal. And they generally have become distinctively American through being regionalists, but you are saying that this was a long and painful process.

Sullivan. One thing bothers me about this. I think that when a writer begins to think, "I'm a Southern writer," he's out of business. There are two points I want to make about this. One is that I was thinking about what the writer really wants to do: he's possessed to tell the truth, as he sees the truth. And I don't think in the case of the Southern renascence the impulse was really to tell the truth about the South. Southern images were what the Southern writer had: he had to write about them. Robert Penn Warren has been going through my head—not his work but his voice—little remarks that he has made. I remember once, right after he had moved to New Haven, somebody asked him, "Red, now that you live in Connecticut are you going to write about Connecticut?" He said, "I can't write about Connecticut. If I get fifty miles out of New Haven, I don't know what people eat for breakfast." This was a very astute remark, you see. If you have to worry about what people eat for breakfast, you don't know them well enough to write about them and probably don't love them enough to write about them or hate them enough to write about them. In another remark he made on an entirely different occasion, he said, "A writer has to feel about his country the same way he feels about his mother, if he's going to write about his country, whether it's the South or New England or the whole nation. He loves her but she annoys him to death." And this seems to be the perfect image. You're loyal and the whole business of loyalty isn't questioned, and you don't have to go into any of these ramifications whatsoever. You know, she's my mother: I'm stuck with her; I'm loyal to her and all this; but, oh, my heavens!, all the things she says and does that she ought not to say and do. And so we live in this tension—it's not a love-hate thing, in a way maybe it is, but of annoyance—annoyance of this thing which you love—and tension develops. This may be a kind of Calvinism.

Now it seems to me that we are living right in the middle of this tension. And we are writing about it. It's like the old joke about the centipede, when another insect came along and said, "My heavens, you've got all those legs, and this is a real accomplishment: it's a tremendous achievement. And how in the world do you synchronize them all?" And he said, "I don't know." And he began to think about it, and he fell over in the ditch. He couldn't walk any more because he'd become too self-conscious. I think this happened to Faulkner really: Faulkner had been sitting down in Mississippi, and I know that he was a man fraught with vanity—there's no question about that, every writer is—and he couldn't have avoided thinking he was damned good; but nonetheless he was so busy writing that he couldn't stop to worry about this, and then finally the moment came when the *New York Times* printed his picture one time too many. Or he opened one letter too many from Malcolm Cowley, or his books sold an extra 1,000 copies, and all of a sudden he said, "I'm a celebrity. And now I've got to live up to it, and being a celebrity, I've got to get with the modern world." And he was finished; he really was. The late Faulkner is just perfectly dreadful.

So it seems to me that all this talk about regional literature is talk that has to take place after the fact. And it may be that when we start to examine it—maybe the very fact that we are examining it—is symptomatic; that the fact of the examination means, "Well, we've got the corpse laid out on the table; it's been safely embalmed; and now we're going to dissect it to see how all the parts work." This is not necessarily a bad thing, but I think we've got to make these distinctions. Here is the writer with a love-hate relationship towards the material he's writing about and really not many theories, not any theories at all probably, trying to get at the truth, trying to tell the thing as he sees it, trying to get the human condition; and on the other hand, the critic coming along after trying to codify what the writers have done. Both of these are legitimate roles. We've got to see them somehow, I think, as two separate roles.

Rubin. Do you think Yeats stopped writing when he started to think about himself as an Irish poet?

Sullivan. Wouldn't you come up with that! This was a peculiar situation though, wasn't it? I mean peculiar in the sense that you had all the violence that doesn't ordinarily attend the sort of thing we are talking about.

Rubin. It just seems to me that what you are saying is simply that any time anyone begins to think of himself abstractly, then to that extent he can't deal directly with his experience. When a Southern writer thinks of himself as a Southern Writer—abstractly—then he sees himself as playing a role. However, I don't think of this as being different from any other writer who may not possess an important regional identity as thinking abstractly about himself. What worries me here is not what you yourself mean, but what so many people who haven't thought about the matter too much mean when they express similar statements: the idea that somehow or other good writers don't *think*—and that when writers start thinking, they're in trouble. Therefore a real writer doesn't sit around and think about theories and so forth and so on. There is a long history of why this kind of anti-intellectual posturing is true: "I'm William Faulkner, just a plain country boy." He's a plain country boy who wrote *The Sound and the Fury*.

For some reason this has never worried the French. Any French writer thinks of himself as perfectly equipped to theorize on literature for as long as he wants, and as often as he wants, without in any way imperilling his professional—or more properly his amateur—status. Writing is a tremendously difficult business, and while it's easy, in terms of this or that glib theory, to explain difficult things, I'm always pretty uneasy when anybody talks about writing as being something in which if once you start to think about it, you're gone. I think it's a tremendously difficult intellectual task, and the man you just mentioned a few minutes ago—Robert Penn Warren—is a marvelous example of the fact that a man can be a very fine conceptual thinker and also a very fine creative writer, and that the two roles are not necessarily incompatible.

Sullivan. That's obviously true. But it's this matter of self-consciousness—when you become self-conscious as a particular kind of writer.

Rubin. Yes.

Sullivan. It seems to me then the thinking becomes a little bit off center.

Rubin. When you think of yourself as filling a role, when you think of yourself not as a writer, let's say, but as a Man of Letters, you get into trouble.

Sullivan. Exactly.

Rubin. I think that's the way it works.

Holman. Isn't this the famous problem of the second novel, if the first one has really been a successful novel? And this is not regional at all: I mean the image and impact of success. The picture the critic has drawn of the writer is there, and somehow he needs to ignore it. It is not that the writer stops thinking about his work and working with his art. It's that he begins thinking about a special role or part which he must play in the literary scene, and this can be a painfully inhibiting thing. I wonder in this respect, though, that since practically all the Southern writers in the last twenty years have vigorously denied that they were Southern writers, whenever they were asked, and have insisted that they don't want that label attached to them, if they're not, in fact, trying to flee from an abstraction which is being imposed upon them by critics and literary historians—and people on panels like this where we're creating an after-the-fact description of a writing. The new writer, if he is really doing his own work, may say, "That's true enough for those boys, but it isn't true for me: I don't belong in that school."

Rubin. Precisely. One of the ways—only one of the ways—by which you will recognize a new Southern writer will be the way in which he is different from what we on a panel can formulate and talk about, and in my case almost make a living out of, as being characteristically Southern.

Sullivan. That's right. There's another angle to this. I think it's a terribly difficult thing now to be a Southerner who wants to write. Assume you were born in Mississippi, that you are living in Mississippi: however much Mississippi has changed and however much your value system deviates from Faulkner's value system, the land still looks the same way, and probably the faces still look the same way, and the weather is the same. Weather is a terribly important thing, and land is a terribly important thing, and water is a terribly important thing. Think how important rivers and lakes are to writers. Nobody writes without using the water symbolism sooner or later. Water symbolism is so much a part of everybody's culture. So every time you look at a river you see the same river Faulkner saw, and he said it better. Don't fool yourself. I mean men like Faulkner come along once every hundred years, if you're lucky; and he said it better, and yet this is yours, this is what you see. And you're bound to be compared with him. Any

Southern writer who publishes books is going to be compared with Faulkner, and it doesn't make any difference if you are as far away from Faulkner as you can get, some critic somewhere is going to say, "This guy was influenced by Faulkner: this guy is trying to write the way Faulkner tried to write." This is the burden, and I think it is a real burden. So there may be some necessity for fleeing to Roxbury, Connecticut, just to see a different land, just to try to get away somehow, out from under the shadow of these giants who have gone over all this ground and have seen it one way, and you've *got* to see it another if you're going to write successfully.

Core. You know this is an incomparable advantage that Shakespeare had—and the Jacobean playwrights had: nobody came along and said, "My, you're writing like Marlowe, or you're writing like Ben Jonson."

Holman. But look at what happened to nineteenth-century drama when the influence of Shakespeare almost destroyed it. So that somehow you need to get free of these tremendous influences, particularly when they've created a whole world. But I would really question, Walter, whether or not the world that Faulkner created—which is his imaginary world, but with real rivers and hills and roads it's true, but still his world with its own cosmology, its own people, and its own problems— whether that world is the world which all Southern writers have to deal with or will deal with. I think that the best thing the writer can do in this particular case is to go about his own business in his own world and when the critic says, "Faulkner," look at him and say, "Who?", and just ignore the type of influence criticism which is inevitably going to come. It follows every *major* work. To a certain extent it's true of the influence of Wolfe. Every Southern writer somehow for a while is a Wolfean writer, if he writes about Wolfe's part of the country. And yet, I think that the real problem is to be free—not from the fact of Faulkner or the fact of Wolfe or the fact of Warren, but from the self-consciousness about other people's view of their work as being work like that of Warren or Faulkner or Wolfe.

Core. Isn't this one thing we've learned, say, with the Milton controversy earlier in this century: that the writers who followed Milton stumbled along in his footsteps, and then Eliot and Leavis came along and said, "Ah, that just proves that Milton was a bad poet." These people had to get out from under Milton just as Mr. Rubin has said writers have had to get out from under Faulkner.

Rubin. Yes, that's true. But, unfortunately, it's not as easy as that. The point is that a lot of writing is much more of an artificial sort of thing than we think. We tend to think, and we tend to see our experience, in terms of what we've read. So if it were simply a matter of not writing under the shadow of Faulkner, this would be fine and very easy to do. And certainly it's true that Faulkner's South is not Walter Sullivan's South. Yet a great deal of Faulkner's South still *is* Walter Sullivan's South. And the job is to get out from under—to do so while still continuing to recognize and use what Faulkner has shown us about looking at our Southern experience. In other words, it's not simply a matter of saying "Faulkner has already done this, so therefore I can't do it. I've got to find my own voice." Faulkner is too good for that: you can't just arbitrarily move away. You can't help but see things his way: because his way of seeing things is partly your way of seeing things too.

Holman. But isn't this what happens when any major literary figure comes along in any language? Every writer who follows him is in a sense limited by what he has discovered and created. And so the further along you are in a literary culture, the more you are shaped, in a sense, and bound by and limited in the use of materials because so many of these materials have become already identifiably the product of someone else.

Sullivan. You've become mighty pessimistic now. That's my role.

Holman. No. Well, we'll swap roles. I don't think this is necessarily pessimistic. I think though that it means that literature has to renew itself in a certain sense by being aware of, and at the same time not being inhibited beyond creation by, these tremendous limits that are upon us. You can never quite describe April as simply and directly and truly as Chaucer did because he did it, and every poet after that has had a little bit of a problem with April. And I think you can find this almost anywhere, and so I don't really believe we are talking about a Southern problem.

Sullivan. I think we are, but in our specific context at this time. Maybe we've got to turn away for a moment—writers have got to turn away from this tradition simply to catch their breath. I may be too acutely conscious of this. I go hunting with some very literate people, and you'd be amazed at how often in a duck blind somebody will see something moving out on the water or over in the rushes that reminds him of something out of Southern literature. It's there, you know, and someone will say, "Look, you remember in Faulkner, you remember that poem by Allen Tate"; and there is no escaping it whatsoever, of course: there it is. And it surrounds you to this extent, you see.

Rubin. Wilde said, "Nature imitates art."

Sullivan. Yes, I know, exactly. The only solution that I could come to was that Southern writers were going to have to turn aside and go another way for awhile. I haven't really written off Southern literature, and I think what is happening in the South now is tremendously dynamic, and I'm referring of course, to—largely to—the social readjustment. And I think, as a lot of other people, both Negro and white think, that the final solution to race questions is going to be found in the South—not in other places. And I think when we can get away from the present and look back on it, that possibly—not for us, not for anybody sitting here—but for some generation of writers who have come in at the tail-end of this experience and have seen it first hand but have also lived beyond it so that the old animosities are no longer being exacerbated but are being healed—at some propitious moment this is going to make some of the best literary material that we've ever had.

We're living in a time of turmoil; the world of the South before World War II is one world, and the South since World War II is another world. I think now is the time for the Southern writer to back off, to keep writing, but for a moment to look in another direction, and to try to bring in another dimension, another angle of the tradition that isn't the woods and the waters, but something else, so that finally we will come back to all this, but in due time—not now.

Holman. Walter, aren't you really saying that there is a tendency when we think as Southern writers or Southern critics or historians, to be a little bit provincial in our thinking? That is, to get ourselves so caught within the framework of the Southern region and its writing that we are not reaching out and touching other things? I notice, for example, in the case of Louis that there was a little period of time when he went through as a critic exactly what you are going through as a novelist. He was telling me that he wasn't going to study Southern literature any more and he wasn't going to do any more writing about it, and so he went off and he wrote a book about Stendhal and Mauriac and a whole group of people like this, and then he came back refreshed and renewed from a new vantage point. He was like someone writing from Roxbury, Connecticut, or Paris, France, about the literature in this region.

Sullivan. Louis really added another dimension to his work, and I think maybe this needs to take place on a general scale as well as on an individual scale, although we've got to do it as individuals.

Rubin. We all tend to think in clichés, and we have to break out of them. We have to play tricks with ourselves all the time as writers, as critics, as everything else, as people too. Yet while it may be necessary at this time or that for a given writer who is a Southerner consciously to think of himself in a different way, to say to himself "I'm not going to think of myself as a Southern writer," and so forth, I insist that there is nothing inherent in the idea itself that makes that kind of denial necessary, but only in the way that people tend to apply it. The term "Southern writer" is used so often in the sense of limitation—of undue limitation, as if there are two separate kinds of writers: Southern writers and American writers. Now it's all right to describe, let's say, John Trotwood Moore or Harry Stillwell Edwards, as a Southern writer in that sense because you're not limiting him—he's already so limited anyway. But if you talk about William Faulkner as a Southern writer, then supposedly you are thereby limiting the importance and the scope and the universality of Faulkner, and I just don't think this is so at all.

The curious thing about literature is that the more concrete a writer's experience is, the more detailed, the more sharply Faulkner writes about people in a single area of Mississippi, the more readable what he has got to say is going to be in Tokyo and Stockholm. So that, in a sense, the more specific he gets, therefore the more universal he becomes. Southern writing is not something apart from American writing: it's simply a very vigorous aspect of the American literary experience. That's why it always makes me a little nervous when people use the term Southern writer as if it constituted a kind of limitation.

Core. The question I was asking earlier is how many American writers are there that didn't write directly out of the region? Hawthorne, for instance, said that New England is as much land as his heart could readily take in. The only one I can think of—major American writer—is Whitman. Is that right, Mr. Holman?

Holman. Well, he's pretty thoroughly tied down, isn't he, except when his imagination starts leaping over mountains and spanning continents, to a section of the coastal Middle Atlantic States and Long Island? The poems of his which seem to speak most emphatically and directly of his own experience—though not of these vicarious adventures—are tied very specifically to a time and a place, though he's obviously trying to be a poet of America—and I think he would be perhaps horrified at this particular discussion that we are carrying on.

Sullivan. What about Hemingway? I know all that Michigan stuff, but it's inferior, really, to the major work. The major work is not American at all in a way: it's the American expatriate: it's the American without a country.

Holman. Henry James is another example of the same thing, for James's American stories are perhaps better than we frequently give them credit for being, but they are certainly not among the major works which he did, though he's usually writing about Americans. We've also got T. S. Eliot, if you'll count him as American.

Core. It seems to me that James and Eliot so thoroughly assimilated the English culture that you're talking about a different situation there, aren't you?

Sullivan. I don't know. It seems to me that Eliot transcends everything in *Four Quartets*. Here he is right in the middle of the war, walking down the street as an air-raid warden, and it's so consequential and so inconsequential at the same time.

Rubin. When I went up to the University of Pennsylvania for a few years, back in the mid-fifties, I found a rather curious thing. When we had talked about experience in the South— and in Virginia and South Carolina, we called it Southern. When I got up there they talked about experience in Pennsylvania, but they didn't call it Eastern: they called it American.

64

They assumed that anything their writers did or thought was American. All other kinds of writers were offshoots, regional offshoots. It has always seemed to me that the culture of the Northeast—I don't mean New England either—is as thoroughly provincial as that of any other region of the country. What made me think about this was the remark about Walt Whitman, who is certainly my favorite American poet. He is, to me, very much tied in with his time and place.

Holman. I think that the point you are making, Louis, is a significant one. I believe it is true that outside the Southeastern United States—except for a little regional self-consciousness that literary groups develop when they have the *Prairie Schooner* or the *Midwest Quarterly* or something of this sort, which are very minor in terms of the total literary scene—you do think of American literature and you think of Southern literature. And there's ample evidence in our history for how *we* came to be this way and how they came to be this way too, if we want to separate we and they. And it is a real hazard which the Southerner has, I believe, because of special aspects of his experience and special attitudes which have grown out of it, a hazard that writers in the rest of the country do not necessarily have. I think, though, that you can turn this around, as a great many people have done many times—and there's no need in going into it here—and see that this is a limitation and handicap, yes; but it is also one of the powerful and strong metaphors out of which Southern writing has been able to be a significant part of the national literature while it retained its regional identity. I think we have retained a regional identity in our writing in a way in which the rest of the country hasn't—a self-conscious regionalism.

Core. You brought up a point, Mr. Sullivan, I'd like to ask you about. We're thinking in terms of the historical period beginning a renaissance, a kind of a cataclysm, which in this case was quite obviously the First World War, and then we are thinking about another one which ends it. And certainly tentatively we agree that the original impulse found its flower and ended about the time of the Second World War—this is something Mr. Holman brought up last night—rather as perhaps the death of the Czarist regime ended the great period in Russia, or as the Puritan interlude pretty well took care of the English theatre. I wonder, do you see the social upheaval as a kind of cataclysmic event right now? It is certainly not a war, but it is something that is affecting the region so thoroughly that it becomes hard to write in the same way that a war would make it hard to write.

Sullivan. It seems to me that the region, the state, the nation, the political entity or the geographical entity no longer demands the first loyalty of most people but that people have other loyalties. That is to say, if you get a division, for example, on the Vietnam war, the people who are against the Vietnam war are first against the Vietnam war, and if you are a native Mississippian who is against the Vietnam war, you have a kinship with a man from New York who is against the Vietnam war. And this would be a first loyalty. This is the way you would identify yourself, and your fellow Mississippians who are *for* the Vietnam war are anathema to you. Now this didn't used to be the case. In the past you would think, "I'm a Mississippian and I identify myself with this region." But now you think, "I am a liberal, I am a conservative, I am for this thing, I am for that thing, and so forth." A lot of political scientists say that nationalism is an out-moded concept. And we simply cannot escape this.

I see this situation as forcing us to come to some different kind of terms with our whole lives and our whole way of looking at the world, and therefore our way of writing about the world. I don't think this new alignment is going to endure forever: I don't think it is necessarily a permanent thing, although a lot of people do. This is particularly true of some Roman Catholic theological writers, and I think of two right off hand—Guardini and Maritain, both of whom say that this division is going to be a very stern and tough division between the forces of good and the forces of evil. Maritain says that the devil is making such a mess of the world it will soon be a place fit only for saints, and that we are going to see at once the greatest manifestation of evil and the greatest flowering of sanctity, side by side, that the world has ever known. Well, this—if your heart will stand it—will be an exciting time to live through; but this is the sort of thing, it seems to me, which is happening so that the old centers of loyalty are breaking down and new centers of loyalty are being developed, and therefore we will have to discover a new way of looking at things, a new way of writing about them.

Rubin. There you are—the apocalyptic thesis all over again now, in a new guise: this is the time of the death of the gods, and everything has completely gone to pot. I imagine that Elizabethan Englishmen went round and worried about things going to pot too and were pretty sure that things were really going to the dogs.

Sullivan. They were too, you know.

Rubin. Sure they were. Now I don't want to be one of these easy optimists, but it seems to me that the times are *always* difficult. Things are always going to the dogs: the young people no longer take heart; the best lack all conviction while the worst are full of passionate intensity; and so forth, and so on. Well, it's been going on for a long time, and somehow I have the feeling that, Maritain or no Maritain, it's going to go on a while longer.

Sullivan. Louis, things do change: reality manifests itself in different ways and loyalties and the bases for loyalties shift. I think that point is germane to the discussion.

Core. So you would say, for instance, although the Irish renaissance is not persisting with the original impact that it did—there are still some awfully good writers over there, producing perhaps a quarter of the *New Yorker's* fiction every year—that these people have still got their loyalty to Ireland essentially intact, whereas Southern writers are shifting their loyalty outside the region.

Sullivan. Well, they are in trouble about that. I'm told that the younger generation of Dublin intellectuals now sneer at the 1916 uprising, that there it is really a little gauche to talk about this and all the old songs and the terrible beauty that was born is all old hat, and I can well believe this.

Rubin. Walter, just let me say one thing about Roxbury, Connecticut. *The Portrait of the Artist as a Young Man* and *Ulysses* and *Finnegans Wake*—they're not your favorite reading, but they were written in Zurich and Paris and Trieste—not in Dublin.

Sullivan. That's true.

Core. They were still written with this intense consciousness of Dublin, weren't they?

Rubin. Oh, yes.

Core. Then it really didn't make too much difference where they were written.

Rubin. No, and that's just the point: Joyce's imagination never left Dublin. All I mean is I just don't think it makes the slightest difference to the writing of Bill Styron that he has moved from Newport News, Virginia, to Roxbury, Connecticut. And I think Walter would write what he writes if he were living in Nome, Alaska.

Sullivan. What a quaint idea.

Holman. I think it does matter that Styron is living outside the South but not necessarily in Roxbury, Connecticut, because as you think back across the Southern writers whom we would include in the group that we discuss in this renascence, was there one of them who did not achieve somehow a physical distancing and detachment before he was able to begin actually producing the work about the South which his fame rests on at the present time?

Rubin. You are absolutely right. Let me clarify what I meant about that business. Of course it makes a great deal of difference to Styron. It makes a great deal of difference to Reynolds Price that he lives right outside of Durham. All I meant is that you can't make any blanket statements about the Southern writer who now doesn't live in the South, and can't write well because he doesn't. So much has to do with the personality of the individual writer. Of course you are absolutely right about this business of detachment. But it need not necessarily be a physical detachment, though frequently it is. William Faulkner's days outside the South were very few, indeed, and not very important. On the other hand, once Thomas Wolfe left, he never came back to live. But in each case there's a tremendous detachment along with a tremendous sense of identification, and both attitudes have to be there.

Core. It seems to me that one point we might explore here is that Mr. Holman was talking about the outer world and novelists that he was considering—especially Stribling who has a wretched prose style, who throws away every good theme and situation he hits upon, who is concerned only with the outer world, and who doesn't ever get into the minds of his characters at all. That's one kind of thing. And on the other hand, perhaps, these people who are so concerned with the inner world have gone too far with technique, and there quite obviously has got to be at some point a merging of these inner and outer worlds.

Sullivan. Right. I think this is really what we've been addressing ourselves to, but how we're going to get there? How—I wish I knew.

Holman. It is in merging the inner and the outer worlds that

Faulkner makes one of his greatest achievements in his early novels, it seems to me. Look at how often his technique deals with what we might call "the problem of perception." Yoknapatawpha County is a very real outer world, so fully imagined that it seems to have an absolute existence. Yet we know that world through the impact it makes on the emotions—the inner selves—of Faulkner's characters. Look at all the major novels—*The Sound and the Fury, As I Lay Dying, Light in August, Absalom, Absalom!*—in every one we see Yoknapatawpha County and its people and its history through the intensely personal and private and often highly inaccurate inner beings of the characters. This is really a very Jamesian approach to fiction, and at his best Faulkner achieves a remarkable balance through its use. As Faulkner once said at the University of Virginia, his method in *Absalom, Absalom!* is "thirteen ways of looking at a blackbird," and the blackbird is there all right, but none of the ways is completely right.

Core. It seems to me that we might say a little something about what Wolfe was doing in *You Can't Go Home Again.* Wasn't he moving in this same direction?

Holman. I think he was certainly trying to move in this direction. It's a question of whether or not, in trying to move in this direction, he was emasculating his talent or whether he was beginning to realize it in a different way.

Sullivan. What do you think?

Holman. I think he was in actual fact moving—I don't think he had gotten there—but I think he was moving toward a new kind of fiction.

Sullivan. I do too.

Holman. And if he had lived to realize this movement, undoubtedly the Wolfe that we would see today—and he could still be a productive man—would be a novelist that we would not be measuring in terms of *Look Homeward, Angel* and *Of*

Time and the River, but in terms of other works of a different type which he had begun attempting to do. At the same time that this is true, I think that Wolfe is an exaggerated example of the writer who's having an enormous difficulty in getting away from his own personal response—the self-expressive theory of art instead of the objective theory; and in the last few years of Wolfe's life I think these two theories were almost in head-on collision in his writing career. In the material he wrote there is a very great unevenness as he shifts between one and the other. He was naturally and by training a romantic with a romantic theory of the imagination—studying with Lowes when Lowes was writing *The Road to Xanadu,* and he apparently never recovered from it. But the need to orient himself to an outside world was increasingly real to him. Now that outside world that he was orienting himself to was an America instead of a South.

Sullivan. The whole world, really.

Holman. Yes, it literally was. It was America, it was Europe, it was the South. And if you take a work like that accumulation—what I on at least one occasion call an anthology—of short stories and short novels, *You Can't Go Home Again,* you find that the primary subjects range over New York, over Europe, over the South; but the general tone is that of a social critic. It's that of a man who is bringing the beliefs and the values of these societies—the Third Reich, the rich in New York, the people in Asheville at the time of the real estate boom—under a kind of satiric scrutiny, which is a quite different kind of satiric scrutiny from that rather simple satire which he addressed to Asheville in *Look Homeward, Angel,* where there is a fair amount too of Sinclair Lewis's type of portrayal of the village. There's a substantially greater depth in the quality of the social criticism of these late works, but it's very fragmentary. None of it's put together in a single piece. If he had decided to do with it what he did with the fragments of *Of Time and the River* and tried to merge it through a single personality or intelligence, he might have lost some of the focus and sharpness that the separate pieces now have.

Sullivan. It seems to me that bit on Germany is as good as anything he ever did. Do you agree with that?

Holman. I think that the three best things that he did were all short novels and self-contained units. I've ranked them in different orders at different times, and without trying to rank them now, I'd say they're *The Web of Earth*, *The Party at Jack's*—or *The House that Jack Built* in its extended version, and *I Have a Thing to Tell You*—the piece about the Third Reich.

Sullivan. Well, now let me ask you, is there any other Southern novelist who did anything comparable to that? I know Faulkner wrote about stuff outside the South, but always it was inferior to his best work. Warren writes a novel like *Wilderness,* and it's distinctly inferior to the stuff he writes about the South. I think Wolfe is unique in this—that he wrote as well about other sections as he wrote about the South.

Rubin. I know that's what Wolfe was *trying* to do. There's no question about that. As to how well he did it, I think we have a little difference of opinion here. I don't think he was quite as successful as you. If you rule out *Look Homeward, Angel,* you take away a large portion of the reason for paying much attention to Thomas Wolfe. *Look Homeward, Angel* is a flawed novel and some of the material towards the end of it is pretty bad, yet it is a major work of the imagination. It is a beautiful novel and it's *Wolfe.* Anything else he wrote is in addition to *Look Homeward, Angel.*

Sullivan. Did any other novelist—any other Southern novelist you know of—write as well about regions outside the South?

Rubin. Well, what would you say about *Set This House on Fire?*

72

Sullivan. What I would say about it is "No."

Core. Perhaps Styron is a case where we can join some of these issues or be broken by them. I was thinking of talking about Styron in these terms—about *Nat Turner*—not *Set This House on Fire.*

Holman. Before we do, I'd like to say just one thing about Louis's remarks on Wolfe, on which I suspect all of us agree. But I would want to point out though that thirty-eight years is not necessarily a short life but was a relatively short career for a writer like Wolfe. And *Look Homeward, Angel* is, in fact, the only really complete piece of work which is Wolfe's that we have. And what we have in these other fragments are simply things which are pointing in directions that he might be going. There's much too much of Perkins in *Of Time and the River,* and there's a lot too much of Aswell in the last two novels. *Look Homeward, Angel* has this peculiar position in Wolfe's career, not only because of its excellence and its Southern subject matter and the effective evocation of childhood in a region, but because it is the one thing that he fully realized in his entire career, which may be a comment on him as well as on something else. But I think it is less germane to the issue of what he was doing at the end.

Rubin. Yes, I think he was definitely trying to do what you say he was trying to do, and I think he was succeeding. I don't know what he would have written if he had lived.

Core. Is part of this irony in those last few books? Is Wolfe finally beginning to look at himself and the outside world simultaneously?

Holman. Well, I think there's irony of a sort. It's fairly heavy-handed, but it's real all through *Look Homeward, Angel.* I think there's an ironic mode that Wolfe writes in very, very frequently. He's refined it some and objectified its subject in the later books. He is less likely to be ironic about himself and more to be ironic about society than he was in the earlier works. Some of the satire in *Look Homeward, Angel* is addressed to the town, but most of the irony is addressed to Eugene, and this irony redeems the book from becoming too overly sentimental.

Core. Mr. Rubin, to get back to Styron for a minute. In his first novel, he's writing very much like Faulkner, isn't he?

Rubin. On the obvious level he's working like Faulkner, but I don't think essentially it is really a very Faulknerian novel.

Core. Yes, but it's not his own voice.

Rubin. Oh, I think it is.

Core. . . . consistently throughout the novel.

Rubin. There are certainly passages in the book which seem very Faulknerian, but it seems to me the Faulknerian business in *Lie Down in Darkness* is immediate and it's obvious—the idiot sister, the alcoholic father, the funeral procession and everything—those things are very definitely Faulknerian. He *said* he started writing it after immersing himself for several weeks in Faulkner. Then he later re-wrote it. Yet I don't think it is really a kind of Faulknerian tragedy, though; I don't think it is a dynastic tragedy in the way the essential Faulkner tragedy tends to be.

Core. What I'm saying is that if we jump ahead to *Nat Turner,* this is the first time Styron has spoken consistently in his own voice and idiom. And in the book you brought up a few minutes ago, *Set This House on Fire,* that the problem again— that Wolfe had too—is the novelist's self becomes confused with his characters.

Rubin. I don't think that *Set This House on Fire* is a flawless novel. I think it's got a serious structural flaw. Yet it is a very fine novel. The novelist does give one character's experience to another. I don't know exactly what that has to do with the South, though.

Core. Well, what about this novel he just finished writing?

Rubin. Mr. Sullivan gave a very interesting analysis of it yesterday. However, I don't agree with the central point of his criticism—which is this business of a character's being anachronistic, of Nat Turner's being not a Negro slave who could read and write and who lived in the 1810s, 1820s and the 1830s in the South but being essentially Stokely Carmichael or Rap Brown put back into that period. This criticism has been made, but I don't really find it a valid criticism myself: I don't find the character unconvincing. For one reason I'm quite sure that the real Nat Turner was not a typical Negro slave. A typical slave couldn't have led the Nat Turner rebellion. I didn't find the so-called anachronistic quality very disturbing. There were times when it was evident, of course: that business about the smell and also the business about the need to maintain a facade before white people and all the self-consciousness with which that was done was undeniably a very self-conscious attempt to see things from the Negro's standpoint. And what the reader sees then is William Styron looking at things from this Negro viewpoint. But for the most part I did not find the style—the sensibility—anachronistic at all, and I found it quite convincing. I found the language of Nat Turner very much the language of the original Nat Turner confession. It may be only the way that Lawyer Gray wrote it: I don't know. But there are certain phrases here and there in the real confession that make me think that it is a much closer transcript of Nat Turner than most people give it credit for being.

Sullivan. I see it as an important problem, but I don't see it as an insurmountable problem. When I wrote the first draft of that paper I read yesterday, I said that this book really should be titled "Confessions of Nat Turner as Written by Leroy Jones and Recited by Stokely Carmichael in the Magnolia County Mississippi Jail." And I think maybe, if it had been done that way, that I would like it very much. We had a little flap in Nashville. Fred Brooks was teaching what he called a freedom school in connection with the O.E.O., and he was having his students in the freedom school re-enact the Nat Turner rebellion. And this seemed to be a perfectly ordinary thing for him to do. Why not?

If you could pick the material up and do it on a double level—both past and present—and do it honestly that way, maybe this would work very well. But obviously the terms Styron gives us are: this is the way it was—so far as he can make it his reconstruction of what happened. This is, after all, what the writer is telling us, isn't it? I'm giving you the essence—the thing as it happened. This bothered me a little bit because I don't think it really did happen this way: it doesn't convince me.

Core. Yet isn't the world itself that he describes here very similar to the world Allen Tate describes in *The Fathers,* or Ellen Glasgow describes in some of her novels? I mean just the texture of the life, the density of the experience.

Sullivan. It seems to me it is and it isn't, and I'm not really prepared at this moment to make that comparison. But I'm not going to stand or fall on this particular issue. I have another objection to the novel. I think it is emotionally un-realized largely until we get to the end of it. I'm moved by the end of the novel, but I'm not moved until we get to the end of the novel, and I think in many ways it is a thin and episodic novel. I don't get a sense—any sort of strong sense—of structure. We are going to move from point A to point B, and it's pretty predictable how we are going to get there. Now this flaw may be built into the material, but even if it is built into the material, a novelist is obligated to over-come the disadvantages that are built into the material, be-cause there are always these disadvantages.

Now right at the end I felt something. Once Nat had killed Margaret Whitehead, the meaning was enhanced for me. This was a significant act. But otherwise the whole thing is a tawdry business, a good deal like a Western novel. Wyatt Earp is coming down one side of the street, and somebody else is coming down the other side of the street, and one of them is going to kill the other one, and that means that we will be simply one step closer to the solution of the Malthusian problem. It means that the undertaker will get a bit of business, that we will have a body to bury, and that all the guy has lost is his life. And this is really of no consequence. The blood-letting never gets significant until the death of Margaret Whitehead. And then it's just too late: too much has happened.

Holman. It seems to me that the issue of whether or not the action of the story—and slavery as an institution, a slave insurrection in 1831, historical or imaginary—is a tawdry matter is not really relevant to the accomplishment of the artist in the book. The thing that matters is what he does with this tawdry matter. And so I'll assume that what you are really saying is that his handling of it does not lift it out of the level of the tawdry. And I think here that in *Nat Turner* the debt of William Styron to Faulkner is still very much present. But it's the debt of a writer who has assimilated to an appreciable extent the methods and processes of another writer, and now in a sense can use them for his own purposes. For I think that Styron does with Nat Turner much the same thing that Faulkner does again and again and again with his illiterate poor whites who could never conceivably ever have said or thought or even dreamed the things, the images, the figures, the rhetoric which Faulkner convinces us that they are actually, unconsciously experiencing in the stories. Styron says this isn't a historical novel—it's a meditation on history, and it seems to me that the meditation here is Styron's meditation, and that in order to make it, he has entered into, or has attempted to enter into, the consciousness of Nat Turner. This is a dangerous strategy, one that is almost doomed from the beginning to be at least partially a failure, and from time to time it fails. But it is a very Faulknerian strategy. I don't mean in subject matter and handling, but it's the way in which Faulkner has, indeed, taken the tawdry. What more tawdry sequence of events, for example, could we think of than that sequence of cheap and violent events that make Wyatt Earp look really rather sophisticated that take place at Sutpen's Hundred in *Absalom, Absalom!* It is what Faulkner's rhetoric, again a rhetoric not his own, he claims, but the rhetoric of his characters, has done in elevating this material and investing it with meaning and with a sort of significance which lifts these very cheap and tiny people in a small and limited community to the stature almost of demi-gods.

Now I don't know how completely Styron succeeded: I think perhaps that, if he could somehow have used a multiple point of view, could have found another means of letting us look at the situation other than Nat Turner's, we might have slackened off a little bit of that perhaps over-realized intensity which the book generates at various points when it becomes a little oppressively over-written. But I really feel that you have to give him credit for attempting something quite different from what you say.

Sullivan. Yes, yes, that's true. One question: what do you think would have happened if he had used the point of view that Warren used in *World Enough and Time* so that you have side by side Bill Styron talking and Nat Turner talking? And Styron speculating, or questioning what Turner did, asking why he did it.

Holman. The books are very much alike in their intention, aren't they? Of course I don't really think that this method would have worked.

Sullivan. I think you are right.

Holman. Because I'll have to confess—and I realize that we differ on this—I don't think it works for Warren either. *World Enough and Time* is an interesting book but ultimately not a successful one. Somehow or other the actions need to be rendered, and if you are going to meditate upon them, you need to find a means of meditating within the terms of the story, not as an author outside the terms of the story. So I wish Styron had found—and I have no idea how he could have done it—some other means of giving us a view of this situation than the means he took—but not his own, not an objective account interspersed with the narrative.

Core. Mr. Rubin pointed out in his paper last night that this religious and moral dimension from Southern literature remains—that it is going to continue to be a vital force, although it may be slightly changed; and I think Styron uses this element very aptly in *Nat Turner*. Do you want to comment on that, Mr. Rubin?

Rubin. Obviously Nat Turner is a preacher who thinks a great deal about God. But one of the things that goes in that novel is his awareness suddenly of the tremendous distance between human interpretations of divine will and any certain knowledge of what divine will is. But I don't think Styron's attitude in presenting this is strictly that of the detached narrator. I think that, essentially, this novel is posited upon religious grounds. I think that not only the meaning but the interpretation of what happens will not make sufficient sense unless this is part of the way of thinking about the novel, and even though Styron is very careful to give everything that happens in that novel a perfectly plausible physiological, scientific basis for action, I don't think that psychological causes are really what make Nat Turner do what he does.

Core. The main impulse is religious, isn't it?

Rubin. I think so.

Core. I would like to ask for questions now, ladies and gentlemen. Mr. Lloyd?

Lloyd. I have heard you all solemnly discuss Thomas Wolfe as a Southern writer. Having lived in Asheville for some fifteen years and never having thought it was the South, having been under the impression that both of Wolfe's grandfathers were on the wrong side during the Civil War—at least one of them was, and thinking of the fact that Wolfe never spoke of Southern institutions with much of anything but contempt—and made tracks to leave Asheville, a cosmopolitan mountain center, as soon as he possibly could, I ask how you call him a Southern writer?

Holman. I have wrestled with this problem before, and I think that, in order to say what you are saying, you have made an assumption that there is a South. I don't know which one you are assuming, but it sounds to me a little bit as though it is located in the Tidewater or low country, and that the South of the Piedmont region is not really a South. Now I would argue that, in actuality, there are many different Souths. I've argued this, in various contexts at various times—that there is a variety of experience in the South. Atlanta certainly is not the South of even Milledgeville, Georgia, or certainly not the South of the country around Augusta at the time that Caldwell was writing about it, or Judge Longstreet, for that matter. And these sections are all a part of this entire region, and I think that your question serves as a warning to us that we have all night been discussing in our own ways and within our own limits our own quite limited concepts of what the South should be.

I think Wolfe wrote a really fine novel about the experience of growing up in the mountains of western North Carolina, that he went back to that experience again in *The Web and the Rock* and described it there from a slightly different angle and with remarkable effectiveness, that he described and commented upon the life of the Southerner—he was peculiarly interested in this problem—the life of the Southerner and the provincial when he follows his path to the big city. And it's almost impossible to look at Wolfe's picture of either Gant or Weber in New York or in Boston without being aware that what he is talking about here is what happens when a

Southern boy, however much he may be fleeing from the South, is experiencing something new and non-Southern. I think Willie Morris's recent book, *North Toward Home,* is concerned essentially with the same problem which Wolfe talked about again and again and again. And I would say, in these terms, Wolfe is a Southern writer, or we are defining Southern writing in extremely restricted terms—which I think most of us do tend to do.

Rubin. He doesn't write like Stark Young, but that doesn't make Stark Young a Southern writer and Wolfe a non-Southern writer.

Holman. I'd say Stark. . . . Well, I'd better not. I was about to say Wolfe is closer to a Southern writer than Stark Young is.

Percy. Each of you gentlemen has had something very interesting to say about regionalism, but I think many of us might still be confused about the distinction between provincialism and regionalism. When does a novelist cease to be merely provincial and begin to be regional? I take it, Mr. Rubin, that you seem to think there is something very good about being regional. You talk about being very specific—and concrete— about the place that was being talked about so that it would be understood in Tokyo or Stockholm or wherever. Is this really the question of what makes Sarah Orne Jewett a provincial writer and Flannery O'Connor a regional writer?

Rubin. There is quite a good essay of Allen Tate's somewhere in his *Collected Essays,* an excellent discussion of just the difference between provincial and regional. I find that almost anything you ever talk about in Southern literature has somewhere been discussed by Allen Tate. What's the difference between provincialism and regionalism, between sectionalism and regionalism? There are various ways of going about it, but the word provincial does, indeed, carry with it at least as far as I'm concerned, the sense of its being an appendage.

A province, after all, is a province of something else. The South was a province; it used to be referred to as a conquered province at one time. It is implicit that provincialism is confined and small and limited, written primarily for itself, for other provincials, concerned only for itself, and not aware of the existence of any place else. So it seems to me that the whole sense of provincial is that of limitation. Regional, on the other hand, does not literally mean that it is an appendage to something else: it does not exist in a subordinate relationship to something else, but it is simply part of a larger whole. So that, to me, when you use the word regional, it doesn't have any connotation of limitation, of lack of awareness, of a smallness of imagination, but is simply a description of the particular form of the imagination and of the awareness. This is the distinction I would make.

Holman. I would agree with everything you've said and want to add that ultimately the test, it seems to me, between provincialism and regionalism in literature, or sectionalism and regionalism, is the test of whether or not the materials of the region are used by the artist in such a way that they have a quality that transcends the limits of the region. And if they do, then we have used a region in a work of art. If they don't, if we are talking about quaint mountain characters in the Appalachians because they are quaint and because they interest us as we rock on summer porches at resort hotels, we probably are being provincial. Local color and regionalism seem to me to be opposing terms in these things.

Rubin. Local color makes no sense unless you think of it in terms of limitation.

Core. What I was trying to get at earlier is that it might well be that this nation is too big for one man to get hold of as a whole. He's got to look at it in terms of a particular region. Miss Nelson?

Nelson. I certainly don't think Faulkner needs any defense from me, but I was rather appalled that you didn't say that at least the late Faulkner is "rather dreadful"—not just dreadful. I cannot believe that the late Faulkner or the early Faulkner or the middle period Faulkner is dreadful. I think it is quite possible that those of us who were reading the late Faulkner were looking for the same sort of thing we were looking for earlier. A man with the intellectual integrity and the sensitiveness that he had was reflecting a different kind of world. In his acceptance speech of a most distinguished literary prize, Faulkner said, "Man shall prevail." This is what I think he is saying in his late writing.

Sullivan. Well, I couldn't agree more that that speech he made when he accepted that prize was a great speech. And I'm sorry that he forgot it so soon. I don't see how you can defend—or how I can defend—the talkie quality of *Intruder in the Dust,* for example. All these lectures that Gavin Stephens makes about how we're going to have to solve the race question. Whatever the nature of those lectures, a novel is action. Now that's not action: that's talk. And I feel the same way about *The Town.* Once Faulkner discovered Gavin Stephens as a mouthpiece, he was gone. He began to tell the world how to operate. I don't think you have to get into whether he was right or not, because he contradicted himself so many times he was bound to be right part of the time. He quit being a novelist and became a preacher. And that's why we think the late Faulkner is bad. I extend his great period on through *Go Down, Moses,* and include in that *The Hamlet* as well as *Go Down, Moses,* and the books I don't like come after. Professor Holman cuts him off even before then.

Rubin. And I do it later.

Sullivan. But you would agree generally.

Rubin. Yes. I happen to think *Intruder in the Dust* is a pretty good novel. It is not as good a novel as *Absalom, Absalom!* and *The Sound and the Fury,* but I wish I had written it. The thing is, though, it isn't whether Faulkner takes a world view, and so forth and so on: that doesn't really make a particle of difference. It's the view that he takes in his fiction, as you say. That's the trouble with the late Faulkner. I thought *The Town* actually was a very funny novel: I enjoyed that; I didn't enjoy *The Mansion:* I thought that was awful.

Sullivan: Wasn't that terrible!

Rubin. In *The Mansion* you have Flem Snopes again. Flem Snopes is Faulkner's arch-villain, and Flem Snopes of *The Hamlet* and similar short stories is a consummately-drawn character. He's a great one at blackmailing. Well, it works fine in the Faulknerian milieu of early twentieth-century Jefferson. But when Flem Snopes steals Linda Snopes's Communist Party card and blackmails her with that, the thing just seems ludicrous. And so much of *The Mansion* seems ludicrous, except for those portions in which he suddenly forgets all about the modern world for its own sake and gets into the description of Mink Snopes who had been in prison for forty years coming back into a world that is strange and moving back towards the town of Jefferson. And that is among Faulkner's very best writing. But there he was back again doing the sort of thing his own milieu made it possible for him to do, and most of the late Faulkner, alas, is not up to that, including, I think, *The Rievers,* which I found a rather dull book.

Core. This in part proves with what Mr. Sullivan said, doesn't it? That Faulkner is no longer comfortable with this world.

Holman. I agree with both these gentlemen, but I think really one of the things that it proves is one of the points that Walter was making very early—that an author who becomes excessively self-conscious about his audience or his role just finds himself suddenly unsure of his communication with his audience. Faulkner certainly begins saying a great many things in his own person or through characters who seem to speak at the moment of their speech as surrogates for him. When he was really creating the great works these things would have been said through the characters and actions of the story without the intrusion of this rhetorical statement. I've often suspected that a part of it was that he had—during the days of *The Sound and the Fury, As I Lay Dying! Light in August, Absalom, Absalom!*—the rather horrified sense of creating these works with practically nobody except Phil Stone listening, and therefore he didn't worry much about the audience. And then suddenly he discovered himself with an audience which he doesn't want to mis-read his story. And so he began writing into his works the things that are in the Nobel prize speech. He didn't discover these ideas when he went to Stockholm: they had been the ingredients of *The Sound and the Fury* and *As I Lay Dying* and these other works—but the implicit artistic ingredients of them, rather than the rhetorical authorial ingredients.

Rubin. The importance of the Nobel prize speech to the work of William Faulkner is not that he gave the speech when he did but that *The Sound and the Fury* and *As I Lay Dying* and *Absalom, Absalom!* are what that speech is all about.

Core. Isn't this the dilemma the American writer always faces? Faulkner may have been better off unrecognized. Maybe Southern writers are better off unrecognized before panel discussions start to work on them.

Holman. Well, it's all right as long as they aren't listening.

Rubin. Yes, I would think so.

Holman. I think that, really, to come back to the point that I was trying to make earlier about that, we do need to separate the act of creativity and the act of historical and critical scholarship. It's thoroughly legitimate for a group of people in the Southeastern United States to study as intensively as they want to the literature of the region. When that literature happens to be as rich as I think all of us on the panel believe the literature of the last half century has been in the South, it's almost obligatory to study it. But in the very act of studying it, the artist himself can suddenly find himself in all sorts of ambiguous relationships to a literary history. And I wonder if maybe T. S. Eliot would not have been a much more productive poet if he had never written those essays on the literary tradition because it was impossible to view literary history the way he viewed it in those essays without beginning to assess himself self-consciously in relation to it.

Rubin. Oh, I don't know.

Sullivan. I don't know either, because I don't see how he could have avoided that, if he were going to arrive at the richness of his knowledge, the simple magnitude of all he brought finally to those last poems, *Four Quartets.*

Johnston. Mr. Rubin, you talked about the religious theme and several have picked it up. Isn't this characteristic of all great literature? This isn't peculiarly Southern, is it?

Rubin. Well, yes and no. Naturally, if you want to look at religion in a certain, very general sense . . .

Johnston. As a theme.

Rubin. I think this is true. I don't think that Dos Passos is a religious novelist in the way that Faulkner is or in the way that Styron is or Wolfe is. I hope that everybody understands that when we talk about Southern literature, and when we assign this or that quality, and say this quality seems to be characteristic of Southern literature, we aren't saying it is true only of Southern literature, or anything like that. I don't think that any of the qualities that are usually assigned to Southern literature are uniquely and purely true of the Southern novel. It happens to be the particular concentration, the congeries of these same values at one time in the work which, in their complexity and their omnipresence together in concert, cause us to recognize the work as identifiably Southern. If you take a basically religious view of the world yourself, then, by the very nature of that viewpoint, I think you would have to say that all novelists—whether they know it or not—are writing from a religious standpoint. I don't really know exactly how to deal with that. All I can say is it seems to me that the values and assumptions that are present in the Southern novel, the way in which the novelists view human experience—its meaning, the way in which they interpret it, the value they give to it, the importance they give to it, are, in my mind at any rate, predicated upon certain absolute religious values which seem to me to be inextricably part of a religious interpretation of experience. I don't think this is as true of many other novelists as it is of the Southerners. But I certainly don't mean that Southern novelists are religious and therefore other novelists aren't religious. From a literary standpoint I think those particular values are conducive to certain qualities of characterization and description and language which produce important, identifiable literary work. The danger of talking about literature in terms of an author's religious position, however, is that you soon begin measuring the literature by other than literary values which I think is a mistake.

Core. Thank you very much, gentlemen.

NOTES

1. This symposium took place as the final session of the Reynolds Symposium at Davidson College on March 19th, 1968. At the end of the discussion questions were asked by the following faculty members: LeRoy Percy and Charles Lloyd, Department of English; Louise Nelson, Department of Economics; and Frontis W. Johnston, Dean of the Faculty.
2. "The New Provincialism," *Collected Essays* (Denver, 1959), p. 292.
3. "The Profession of Letters in the South," *Ibid.*, p. 281.

A Crossing of the Ways:
AN AFTERWORD
GEORGE CORE

SOUTHERN literature is the most various, complex, and vital response to human experience in the United States in this century. Indeed the Southern literary renascence is the most powerful "rebirth" in letters in the twentieth century, excepting the Irish renaissance, which got well underway in the nineteenth. This would still be true had William Faulkner never written a word, much in the same way the English renaissance would be the most significant period in English literary history without the towering presence of Shakespeare. Both periods would be considerably diminished, of course, without these abiding presences; and without Faulkner Southern literature might still be largely unrecognized outside its region. But the fact remains that the enduring importance of modern Southern literature does not simply rest upon the greatness of William Faulkner—or Thomas Wolfe, for that matter.

Southern literature since the twenties contains all these elements which have been articulated in the essays and the symposium contained in this volume, and there is no need to restate them here even in passing, since they have been dealt with persuasively by all three contributors not only on this occasion but many others[1]—and by a number of other perceptive commentators. It is worth noting, however, that the influence of James Joyce and the impact of aestheticism on the Southern renascence have not been examined earlier—and that the social issues which one associates with the Midwestern renaissance of the early twentieth century have never been truly evaluated in Southern fiction. Both matters are of considerable interest and significance in and of themselves—and because they demonstrate that the literature of the modern South has been markedly affected by observable outside influences which contribute to its universality and continuing importance. Most of the studies written thus far on this remarkable period have dealt with nature of the region—and the texture and tone of its life, and this body of criticism and scholarship has been largely devoted to the rediscovery of eighteenth- and nineteenth-century writers like Byrd, Simms, Poe, Longstreet, Lanier, Harris, Cable, and Mark Twain. The interest in the South (both within and without the region) has been renewed and tempered as a result, and it has also begun to take on the kind of Arnoldian detachment that Louis Rubin argues is absolutely necessary for a true and full evaluation. Yet too often that study has been limited to the South itself: perhaps too much has been done with the influence of Harris and Twain on Faulkner, perhaps too little (as Mr. Rubin implies) with that of Chaucer and Cervantes. So it may be that we need to turn to these and other matters—to the influence of Joyce and Sinclair Lewis, for instance.

There are other problems which have been wrestled with in the course of this symposium, and many are unanswerable. As C. Hugh Holman observes in his essay, "The occurence of genius, even of high talent, is finally inexplicable." And Richard Weaver once said in this connection: "Literary genius, like gold, is where you find it, but when the vein is exhausted, there isn't any more."[2] In a distinctive and powerful literary period there are the incidence of genius—and high talent— and the coincidence of the moment: such an intersection— what Allen Tate has called a "crossing of the ways"[3]—is rare, and it must inevitably pass after a time, perhaps a generation

—or be renewed by other impulses. These forces may engender a counter-renaissance, in the way that metaphysical poetry was a brilliant reaction to conventional Elizabethan verse, or that Jacobean drama in the early days (from 1603 to 1625) was an equally brilliant reaction to the Tudor history play and revenge tragedy. In both the original current and the subsequent cross-current there is an element of radical change together with a less distinguishable (but still important) dimension of continuity. We ignore the latter only at the peril of oversimplification.

So the Southern renascence has much in common with earlier literary epochs of concentration.[4] (This particular epoch is of course more properly a birth than a rebirth, even as is the New England renaissance, since no considerable body of good New England literature existed before 1830, or good Southern literature before 1920.) It resulted in large part from the forces which were loosed by the First World War, a cataclysm of the kind which Matthew Arnold calls an "animating event." The United States briefly gave up its isolationism and became a part of the world, and the South again became a part of the nation. The South maintained its regional identity and its sense of the old ways, however, and not long thereafter its writers began to draw simultaneously upon its rich mythology and react to the powerful literary forces being generated in England and on the continent in the work of Yeats, Pound, Eliot, and Joyce. (Soon also they were to react—less favorably—to the "lost generation.")

If Southern writers could not ignore the impact of modernism, neither could Southern citizens ignore the tremendous impact of the depression when it came a decade later, although they were in a sense psychologically prepared for it as a consequence of reconstruction and were affected less than the remainder of the nation since their economy was agrarian. Southern writers were able in the presence of this great cultural shock to recapture the romance and agony of the past, a past which contained its own animating event and turning point—the Civil War. It is a cause for wonderment that the best Southern writing of any time took place during the depression when writers in the remainder of the country were embroiled in matters of topical "relevance." (Faulkner's great period falls squarely in the most extreme part of the depression.) The renascence in the South really began as American innocence faded once and for all on the stock exchange, and by 1929, an enormously productive literary year throughout the country—but especially in the South, it was well underway. The original movement ended during the forties as the Second World War raged towards its conclusion, and there was a final moment of fruition in 1946.

The flow of Southern writing is greater than ever before as each year passes since that time, and some of it has been very good indeed as Mr. Rubin has said. If the great days are over, there is still much good literature being published, although one must ask if there is enough that is first-rate for us to call this period a continuing renascence. If the renascence does continue, one must acknowledge that much of its vigor since 1946 comes from the writers who began it in the first place: Faulkner (in *Intruder in the Dust* and *The Town*), Warren (in *Brother to Dragons* and *Promises*), James Agee (in *A Death in the Family*), Katherine Anne Porter (in "Holiday" and *Ship of Fools*), Donald Davidson (in *The Long Street*), and Andrew Lytle (in *The Velvet Horn*).

One is struck by the fact that these examples are principally fiction, and Mr. Rubin's list of recent Southern literature is restricted to fiction. Our discussion in the symposium is also limited to Southern fiction, although we made no prior agreement in this regard. Indeed, Southern fiction today is clearly superior to Southern poetry, although there are fine young poets like James Whitehead and Dabney Stuart and good ones of an older generation like Miller Williams and James Dickey. Southern poetry today is in many respects "indistinguishable from that in the rest of the country," as Richard J. Calhoun has recently suggested.[5] One might add that this has been so since Randall Jarrell's generation. Fugitive poetry has not exercised a demonstrable influence on subsequent Southern poetry even though Whitehead, Williams, Dickey, and other contemporary poets studied at Vanderbilt—and because on the whole contemporary Southern poetry does not indicate the concert of techniques and values which are characteristic of Southern writing. These poets are generally more cosmopolitan and less autochthonous than their literary forebears. They are also less inclined towards criticism, even though they are associated with universities in the South.

The present state of Southern poetry results in part from a predictable reaction to the poetry and criticism of Ransom, Davidson, Tate, and Warren; it is also in larger part an aspect of the direction that the main stream of American poetry is taking at the present time. The principal current of verse today in and out of the South is quite obviously romantic: it follows the line of Emerson, Whitman, Williams, Stevens, and Roethke—not Taylor, Emily Dickinson, Eliot, Ransom, or even Wilbur. If Tate and, to a lesser extent, Ransom and Warren have profited immensely by the example of Eliot, few poets in the recent past seem to be directly influenced by his ironic metaphysical style. On the whole, there is not the fusion of critical and poetic practice that one finds in the New Critics, even though poets like Williams and Dickey are much interested in criticism and write fine criticism from time to time. Altogether one feels justified in saying as Ransom did in 1935 that poetry today which is identifiably Southern lacks a sufficient aesthetic and that it is not so mature as Southern fiction.[6] Contemporary Southern poets have reacted against the Fugitive poet-critics, but thus far they have largely failed to create a theory of art and life which one encounters in *I'll Take My Stand, God Without Thunder, The World's Body, Attack on Leviathan,* and *Reactionary Essays.*

In 1954 Andrew Lytle commented a little ruefully that the "continuing renascence" involved many writers who were still very much alive but who had turned away from creative work to the writing of criticism. He said then, "this flux of critical display seems to me the only evidence of mortality."[7] In the last fifteen years Caroline Gordon, Tate, Davidson, Ransom, Warren, and Lytle himself have turned some of their finest efforts to criticism, and today there is great evidence that younger men in the South have learned the lessons of the New Criticism. Yet one hastens to say that the criticism of Tate, Brooks, Warren, and Ransom is not as good as it was—and that the South no longer dominates the literary world as it once did in the early days of the *Southern Review.* There is plenty of good criticism, yes; but relatively little preeminently good criticism. Of course, this is still an epoch of expansion—a critical age.

(One notes in passing that there has always been a decidedly limited amount of good drama in this country. The theatre in the United States—as in England—has yet to recover from the Puritan interlude. Therefore the scarcity of Southern drama is part and parcel of a national failure.)

This is all to say that the Southern renascence is continuing mainly through its fiction, through the form of art which has always been the most distinctive in the South. Fiction, far more than poetry, depends upon social convention. And its principal subject is manners, manners which ultimately profess moral attitudes, directly or indirectly. The novelist must create a whole world in the course of his fictive encounter with reality, whereas the poet can be content with a glimpse into a single mind. The poet is accordingly freed from certain constraints, while being more specifically bound by technical considerations, in a theoretical sense at least. The lyric poem is made to be looked at from without, but the novel has to be seen from within in terms of its own social and metaphysical limits and order. Hence the novelist is more dependent upon a culture for the shaping force of his imagination to be actively engaged.

In the United States culture is largely a regional matter due to the complexion of national growth and development since colonial times. If the regional identity is lost—or the identity of a cultural group like the Jews, the artist writing out of a particular background may find himself in the same position that Donne uneasily occupied when the Elizabethan world picture was shattered, and such awkward transitional periods are largely barren for the epic poet and the novelist. Mr. Sullivan believes this kind of extreme fragmentation and radical transformation has been occurring in the South since the end of World War II. Mr. Rubin's rebuttal is that his position is founded upon cultural and religious argument far more than it is a literary one. Yet the opposite point of view—that the South is largely maintaining its regional identity and awareness—is also largely cultural (and sociological) in its focus, and in both cases the critic finds himself on uncertain ground.

There is no right answer here—and no solid middle ground; moreover, one can have considerable sympathy, as I do, for both approaches. My own uncomfortable feeling is that Southern writers must somehow avoid the literary decadence which is all too clearly on the horizon. The skillful use of language today—the hard polished style—and the more arresting uses of technique are often facile in the worst sense and hence meretricious. I rather suspect we need a new primitivism, a return of the real material of art, with a concomitant sense on the maker's part that the most fundamental human experience never changes, even though it may issue forth (like art) in different forms and attempt new orders.

At the moment the Southern novel may be in the same position as tragedy in Beaumont and Fletcher's time: it has enough brilliance of technique to carry off an action that is confused and morally unclear—or empty. Styron's *Set This House on Fire* is a fair example, despite its technical flaws; whereas his recovery in *The Confessions of Nat Turner* may or may not indicate a continuing resurgence in his own work—and in the region.

One thing is immediately clear, however: there is presently no Yeats or Eliot, no Joyce or Faulkner in sight in the South. And this seems a bad sign. Every renaissance has had its great genius, and this one, in its continuing manifestations, can hardly be an exception. Furthermore, there is a real question as to whether a figure of preeminent literary gifts can go his own way in the United States today without being derailed or corrupted by popular adulation, even as Faulkner probably was in the end. The presence of a great genius would seem necessary for the contemporary Southern renascence to be generated by new energy—and for it to go its own way rather than be carried simply by the force of reaction. One remembers that the English renaissance ended for all practical purposes with the deaths of Donne and Jonson: not even Milton could renew it. And the Irish renaissance effectively ended with the deaths of Yeats and Joyce.

Finally one can only speculate. The value of this symposium as a whole, as Hugh Holman has remarked to me, is not that it definitively answers the questions but that it clearly frames the issues. The collision of the several formulations in the discussion and the resulting stalemate show that the issues can be pondered but not resolved once and for all. And, one may conclude, the work of the artist—and the critic—always involves a tentative formulation about the nature of reality. The artist may continue the work of God, as Blake said, but he never finishes it—so too his critic.

NOTES

1. See, for example, Walter Sullivan, "The Decline of Regionalism in Southern Fiction," *Georgia Review*, XVIII (1964), 301–308, and "In Time of the Breaking of Nations: The Decline of Southern Fiction," *Southern Review*, IV, n. s. (1968), 299–305; C. Hugh Holman, *Three Modes of Modern Southern Fiction* (Athens, 1966); Louis D. Rubin, Jr., *Writers of the Modern South: The Faraway Country* (Seattle, 1963) and *The Curious Death of the Novel* (Baton Rouge, 1967); and essays by all three men in *Southern Renascence* (Baltimore, 1953) and *South* (Garden City, 1959), ed. Louis D. Rubin, Jr., and Robert D. Jacobs.

2. Letter to Randall Stewart dated Chicago, June 25, 1956. Quoted by the kind permission of Mrs. Polly Weaver Beaton.
3. "The Profession of Letters in the South," *Collected Essays* (Denver, 1959), p. 281.
4. This is Matthew Arnold's term; it and the other references to Arnold are taken from his "The Function of Criticism at the Present Time" (1864).
5. "Southern Voices: Past and Present," *Southern Review,* IV, n. s. (1968), 490.
6. "Modern with the Southern Accent," *Virginia Quarterly Review,* XI (1935), 199–200.
7. "A Summing Up," *Shenandoah,* VI (1955), 28–29.

NOTES ON THE CONTRIBUTORS

C. Hugh Holman, who has been Dean of the Graduate School and Faculty Provost.at the University of North Carolina, is Kenan Professor of English at that university. Professor Holman is currently writing a biography of William Gilmore Simms under the auspices of a John Simon Guggenheim Memorial Fellowship. He is editor of *The Thomas Wolfe Reader, The World of Thomas Wolfe, The Letters of Thomas Wolfe to His Mother,* and *The American Novel Through Henry James.* Mr. Holman wrote the Thomas Wolfe number for the University of Minnesota Pamphlets on American Writers, and his *Three Modes of Modern Southern Fiction* was published by the University of Georgia Press in 1966.

Louis D. Rubin, Jr., is now professor of English at the University of North Carolina after having taught at Hollins College for ten years. Some eight books dealing with Southern literature and culture have been written or edited by Mr. Rubin. His most recent books are *The Curious Death of the Novel, The Hollins Poets,* and *The Teller in the Tale.* Professor Rubin is editor of the Southern Literary Studies series published by the Louisiana State University Press, and he is presently editing a bibliographical checklist of Southern writers for that press. He is also editing a new periodical with Mr. Holman, the *Southern Literary Journal.*

Walter Sullivan has been a member of the faculty of Vanderbilt University since 1948 and professor of English since 1959. Two of his novels have been published—*Sojourn of a*

Stranger (1957) and *The Long, Long Love* (1959), and he has recently completed a third. Professor Sullivan has held a *Sewanee Review* Fellowship for fiction writing and a Ford Foundation Grant. Like Holman and Rubin, Sullivan has contributed widely to various quarterlies; and he reviews fiction regularly for the *Sewanee Review*. Mr. Sullivan is a short story writer as well as a novelist and critic.

George Core joined the faculty of the University of Georgia in June after having taught at Davidson College. He edited a collection of Randall Stewart's essays, *Regionalism and Beyond,* which was published earlier this year, and he is co-editor of two forthcoming books—*The Southern Tradition at Bay* by the late Richard Weaver and a collection of critical essays on Katherine Anne Porter. Mr. Core has written essays and reviews for a number of Southern journals, including the *Georgia Review* and the *Southern Review*.

Index

Frank, Joseph, 7
Freeman, Douglas Southall, viii
Fugitive, 21
Fugitives, ix, 35, 92

Genet, Jean, 10
Glasgow, Ellen: viii, 25, 35; and
    Styron, 76
Gordon, Caroline, viii, 93
Gotterdammerung theory, 11
Grady, Henry W., 17
Green, Paul, viii, 35
Grotesque, 28, 30
Guardini, Romano, 66

Hawthorne, Nathaniel: 63; and
    Flannery O'Connor, 29
Heilman, Robert: 39; quoted, 36
Hellman, Lillian, viii, 35
Hemingway, Ernest: 12; as ex-
    patriate, 64
Heyward, Dubose, 35
Hoffman, Frederick J., 36
Holman, C. Hugh: 95; quoted, 89;
    on Wolfe, 37

Irving, Washington, 53

James, Henry, 64
Jarrell, Randall, 92
Jefferson, Thomas, 46
Jewett, Sarah Orne, 81
Johnston, Frontis W., 86
Jones, Madison: *An Exile,* 1–5; *An
    Exile* and Styron's *Nat Turner,*
    1–5
Jonson, Ben, 59, 95
Joyce, James: 15, 18, 68, 88–89,
    90, 95; influence on Wolfe, 22,
    25; "The Dead," 9; *Finnegan's
    Wake,* 9; *A Portrait of the*

Artist as a Young Man, 5–11;
    A Portrait and Marlowe's
    Faustus, 7–10

Kafka, Franz, 52
Kelley, Edith Summers: *Weeds,*
    24–25

Lanier, Sidney, 89
Leavis, F. R., 60
Lewis, Sinclair: 21–22, 89; *Main
    Street,* 22, 26; and Wolfe, 71
Lloyd, Charles, 79–80
Local color: and regionalism,
    53–54, 82
Longfellow, Henry Wadsworth,
    53
Longstreet, Augustus Baldwin,
    80, 89
Lost generation, 90
Lowell, James Russell, 53
Lowes, John Livingston: and
    Wolfe, 71
Lytle, Andrew: 35, 91, 93; quoted,
    92–93

McCullers, Carson, 35
Mailer, Norman, 10
Maritain, Jacques, 66–67
Marlowe, Christopher: 51, 59;
    *The Tragical History of Dr.
    Faustus* compared to Joyce's
    Portrait, 7–10
Mauriac, Francois, 62
Mencken, H. L., 21, 34
Midwest literature, 54, 89. *See
    also* Lewis, Sinclair
Midwest Quarterly, 65
Milton, 60, 95
Mitchell, Margaret, 16
Moore, John Trotwood, 33, 63

Moore, Merrill, 35
Morris, Willie, 81

Negro: and the South, x, 11, 19, 31–32, 41, 47, 51, 61
Nelson, Louise, 83
New Critics, ix, 92–93
New Masses, 25
Northeast: the culture of, 65

O'Connor, Flannery: 13–14, 27–29, 29–32 *passim,* 81; "The Displaced Person," 28; *A Good Man Is Hard to Find,* 28; and the grotesque, 28, 30; and Hawthorne, 29; *Wise Blood,* 31
Odum, Howard, 17

Page, Thomas Nelson, 16
Percy, LeRoy, 81
Percy, Walker, 48
Perkins, Maxwell: and Wolfe, 73
Piedmont South: and Wolfe, 37, 80
Poe, Edgar Allan, 89
Poetry, 35
Porter, Katherine Anne, viii, 91
Pound, Ezra, 90
Prairie Schooner, 65
Price, Reynolds, 69
Provincialism: and Southern literature, 33. *See also* Regionalism

Ransom, John Crowe: viii, 92–93; quoted, 39, 50
Rahv, Philip, 10
Reconstruction, ix
Regency-Hyatt, 31

Regionalism: in American literature, 52–54, 63–65, 82, 93–94; and provincialism, 81–82; and Southern literature, 54–56
Renaissance: 65–66; counter-renaissance, 90; English, 95; Irish, 67–68, 88. *See also* Midwest literature
Renascence, Southern: characteristics, ix–xii, 11, 19–20, 31–32, 36, 38–41, 88–91; continuance, 13–15, 31–32, 41–50; 66–68, 94–95; criticism, 36–38, 92–93; fiction, 93; poetry, 91–92. *See also* individual authors, Regionalism
Roberts, Elizabeth Maddox, 35
Roethke, Theodore, 92
Roman Catholicism: and Flannery O'Connor, 13–14, 28–29
Roosevelt, Franklin Delano, 17
Rubin, Louis D., Jr., viii, 18, 31, 60, 62, 89, 94

Shakespeare, William, 19, 51, 59, 88
Simms, William Gilmore, 34, 53, 89
Social criticism: in Southern fiction, 20–32 *passim,* esp. 30–32
South: agrarian society, 11, 19, 20, 31–32, 47; before and after World War II, 62; "decline and fall" of the Old South, 45–48; many Souths, 16–18, 80; urban South, 31–32, 47–48. *See also* Negro
Southern fiction: *See* individual authors; Renascence, Southern; Style
Southern literature: religious aspect, xi, 11, 31, 36, 47, 52, 86–87. *See also* individual